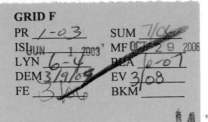

LIVING IN SHADOWS

How to Help the Stray Cat in Your Life (without adding to the problem)

Ann K. Fisher

Amythyst Publishing, Los Angeles, California

Living in Shadows
How to Help the Stray Cat in Your Life
(without adding to the problem)

By Ann K. Fisher

Published by Amythyst Publishing
PO Box 65021
Los Angeles, CA 90065-0021
http://www.livinginshadows.com

Printed in the United States of America
10 9 8 7 6 5 4 3 2 1

Library of Congress Control Number: 2001 127024
ISBN: 1-931395-00-4

Disclaimer

This book is designed to provide information about the subject matter covered. It is sold with the understanding the publisher and author are not engaged in rendering legal, accounting or other professional services. If legal or other expert assistance is required, the services of a competent professional should be sought.

It is not the purpose of this manual to reprint all the information that is otherwise available on the subject, but to complement, amplify and supplement other texts. For more information, see the references in the Appendix.

Every effort has been made to make this book as complete and as accurate as possible. However, there may be mistakes both typographical and in content. Therefore, this text should be used only as a general guide and not as the ultimate source of cat information. Furthermore, this manual contains information on cats only up to the printing date.

The purpose of this manual is to educate and entertain. The author and Amythyst Publishing shall have neither liability nor responsibility to any person or entity with respect to any loss or damage caused or alleged to be caused directly or indirectly by the information contained in this book.

If you do not wish to be bound by the above, you may return this book to the publisher for a full refund.

Dedication

To Chuck, a stray and my first cat. Chuck made his debut as a tiny kitten that could fit in the palm of my hand. He ran up to me on the street, got my attention with a plaintive mew, and within 24 hours had won my heart. It was Chuck who dispelled for me the myth that cats are aloof and uncaring. Without Chuck, I would never have discovered the fascinating world of cats.

Chuck

Acknowledgments

Thanks go to Best Friends Animal Sanctuary, and especially Faith Maloney who gave me insights into the world of homeless animals, Diana Asher for sharing her expert cat knowledge, and Jean Morris who set up the interviews and the times spent with the feral cats at the sanctuary; to the San Francisco SPCA for allowing the reprint of their "Cat Rights;" to Heart of the Earth Marketing for allowing the use of the trap picture; to Norma Behesnilian for the use of the picture and her expertise on feral cat taming; to Stephen Loeb for help with editing and proofing; to my daughter Christina Sanchez for her continued support; and to my editor, Carolyn Porter for all her help.

About the Author

Ann Fisher has been an animal lover and pet owner of dogs, cats and horses since childhood. She has been caring for stray and feral cats, and has also been able to tame a few well enough to keep as "inside" pets. When she first started feeding stray and feral cats, she knew the importance of spaying and neutering pets but was unsure of what to do with the stray and feral cats. Although Ann lives in a major city, she found there was no humane information or help for the feral cats from the local shelters. After several years of practical experience and extensive research, she felt compelled to write a resource to share with others who want to care for feral and stray cats. Ann says, "Although I cannot touch some of the cats, and some cats I feed are so wild I rarely even see them, I still find I get great satisfaction from helping them and having the chance to watch these fascinating creatures." Her hope is to help the reader enjoy this same experience.

Ann Fisher and Chuck

Contents

Foreword

One of my first experiences with feeding a feral cat was Simon. At least that's what I called him—he never told me his real name.

Simon turned up outside my house one day. I trapped him and got him neutered, then let him back out to live his own kind of life. He was a seal point Siamese mix with wild blue eyes.

He loved his life. I created an enclosed feeding station for his food and water, and an insulated house with a blanket for chilly days and nights, and left the rest up to him. He would disappear for several days, and I was afraid that he might have met a bad end, but then he would turn up looking sleek and proud of himself after his wild adventures that I would never know anything about.

He showed all the cunning and strategy of a wild animal, avoiding unpleasant contact with dogs—by deftly jumping out of range—should one come by. He would tempt them into frenzied barking from the branch of tree, while calmly grooming himself from chin to toe. He was a super cat and he knew it.

He lived a free life for over eight years, and then one day he left and never came back. He was beginning to slow down, so perhaps a coyote got the better of him. I'll never know, but what I do know is that he was a complete and fulfilled cat. He never let me touch him, even though I got close a few times, but we shared some time together. I felt honored to have known him.

Ann Fisher, in her book *Living in Shadows*, invites us all to participate in this experience with good solid information about taking care of those cats that live on the fringes of society.

On a recent visit to Atlanta, I helped a friend with her daily feeding of a colony of cats that had congregated behind her office building. As we drove into the parking lot, loaded down with paper plates and canned and dry cat food, cats of all shapes, sizes and colors came running from everywhere, meowing up a storm. We hurriedly opened up the cans, in response to their noisy greetings. Soon the parking lot was blessedly quiet, as they chowed down as if they had never seen food like it before. (They had—the day before! It is like this everyday.)

My friend had trapped, then spayed or neutered the whole group and kept track of them all by name. She pointed out the moms and their grown-up kittens, and the old tomcats with tattered ears and thick jowls. They were her pride and joy, as much loved as her cats at home.

Taking care of feral cats is a rewarding experience, not only for the cats but for all the caretakers too. I hope this book will lead you to share some of your time and resources to help all those cats that live in the shadows.

Faith Maloney
Director Animal Care
Best Friends Animal Sanctuary

Introduction

"It's not my cat, I just feed it."

How many of us have said this about a stray cat we feel sorry for and start feeding? Yet, the stray cat that comes to your door day after day to be fed has a way of working herself into your heart. You really do care about the cat and what happens to her.

You may not be able to bring the cat into your home. You may already have a cat or cats indoors, or a dog that does not tolerate cats. You may not be able to have an indoor cat because of allergies, or other factors. Or the cat may be too wild to want to come indoors and be happier remaining outside full time.

The author believes that cats are best being indoor only pets. However, there is a tremendous overpopulation of cats, of which many are killed each year by starvation, road accidents or by being turned into animal "shelters" where they are killed if not adopted within a few days.

The good news is that you as an individual can directly and effectively help stray and feral cats.

That is what this book is about, ways you can enjoy stray and feral cats as pets while helping to reduce the number of homeless cats.

Advantages of a Feral or Stray Cat

Although you don't really own a feral cat in the traditional way we think of owning a pet, they can make good pets. If you have a maximum number of household cats, a feral cat or cats can be additional "pets" without overstressing the indoor cats you already have. After a time, some feral cats can be tame enough to allow you to pet them gently and may learn to meow for food when they see you. Some will even become tame enough over time to allow you to pick them up.

If you have allergies, feral cats can be ideal pets. The cats stay outside, and contact with them is minimal.

You can have more feral cats than household cats. Although there are limits to the space in your yard or neighborhood, more can live outdoors than you can have in your house.

Cats are interesting to watch. The cat's ability to leap effortlessly onto high places, keen sense of hearing and sight invite our admiration. The feral cats I keep as outdoor pets know when I arrive home and wait patiently for me to come out and feed them, just like my indoor housecats wait to greet me inside my front door.

The author is one of the estimated 17 million people feeding stray and feral cats, not a cat "expert." Speaking from personal experience:

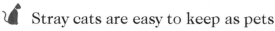 Stray cats are easy to keep as pets

Helping stray cats by feeding them is not difficult

🐈 Stray cats each have an individual personality, a social structure, and are entertaining to watch

🐈 Stray cats, and cats in general, have much to teach us about life

This is what this book is about—simple ways you can help stray and feral cats including:

🐈 Feeding

🐈 Spay and neutering to end the overpopulation

🐈 Habitat improvement, if necessary

🐈 Health care

🐈 Day to day management

🐈 Taming and orphan kitten care

An appendix with names and addresses of organizations for help when you need it, as well as other books and resources on stray and feral cats is included.

The book is setup to read straight through if you wish to know everything about feral and stray cats in the order that events normally progress. If you have a specific interest or problem, you can go directly to the chapter you need most at that moment. Each chapter is independent of the others.

So, without further ado, let's get started with how to understand and help our feline friends.

Cat Beginnings

*I*t will not be a surprise to any cat lover that the origin of the cat-people relationship is somewhat mysterious. No one is really sure where domestic cats originated.

The modern domestic cat is the official name of the cats we are referring to in this book: whether the cat is a pampered purebred cat, a random bred stray or feral cat, they are all included in the species known as the domestic cat or Felis catus.

The modern domestic cat, Felis catus (sometimes referred to as Felis domesticus), is part of the larger cat family, Felis that also includes the big cats of today. Cats occurred on every continent but Australia, and have thrived in most parts of the world at one time or another.

Cats are total carnivores, shown by the short skull length giving them jaws that are more powerful to aid in hunting. Both hearing and vision are a cut above the dog, but the dog has a little better sense of smell.

How Did the Cat Become Associated with People?

The most important event leading to the domestication of animals was when people began growing and storing grain. The only animal domesticated before people started growing crops was the dog, which helped man with hunting.

Grain in abundance attracted cattle and sheep and they became domesticated. The grain also attracted grain-eating rodents. The cats came for the rodents, a major food source, and probably for the refuse as well. We see proof of how well cats do at scavenging today in the swelling number of feral cats.

It is sometimes said that humans found the cat to be of value for its ability to hunt rodents. Another way of looking at it is the rodents found the grain storage to be an ideal food source. Then the cats found the rodents who ate the grain to be an ideal food source, with human refuse as an added incentive.

It is not clear whether the cats adopted people or people adopted the cats. Many times even today it seems that a stray or feral cat adopts a person rather than the other way around.

Who are the Domestic Cat's Ancestors?

The most recent theory is that the domestic cat has three probable ancestors: the African wild cat (Felis silvestris libyca), the forest wild cat (Felis silvestris), and the Asiatic desert cat (Felis silvestris ornate). The foremost ancestor of the modern domestic cat is the African wild cat. The reasoning for this is that the

African and Asiatic wild cat's kittens are both easily tamed while the forest wild cat's kittens are not. The most compelling evidence in favor of the African wild cat is that the domestic cat first appeared in ancient Egypt, the territory of the African wild cat.

The Cat in Ancient Egypt

Egypt may have been the highest point in history for cats. The Egyptians considered the cat to be a valuable asset. They were worshiped by the Egyptians and mummified when they died. In 1889 a large number of cat mummies were discovered in rows in a cavern in Egypt. There were so many that they were considered of little value and most were sold for fertilizer, leaving very little for later studies on the Egyptian cats.

The Egyptians guarded their cats from outsiders and rarely let them leave the country. When the Romans conquered Egypt around 30 BC the cat began to spread out slowly throughout the Roman Empire. The cat reached Europe and England around 5 AD. Cats were almost certainly rare, and only the rich would have kept them as pets.

Cats in Europe

In the early days of Christianity in Europe, the cat was the only pet allowed in monasteries and convents. But as time progressed and the cat became more common in the Middle Ages, people no longer held cats in high regard. Cats, most likely feral, were sometimes chased in the hunt. The cat's fortune continued to go downhill with the Christian Church's witch-hunt. Cats were associated with witches and devil worship. Cats were burned alive in towns all over Europe during the witch trials. Gradually the Age of Reason came into being and cats became less persecuted.

In the nineteenth century cats became popular as pets. The cat fancy or breeding of pedigreed cats and cat shows began. The first cat show was held in 1871. Cats' popularity as a pet has increased steadily until today.

The Cat Today

Today the cat is the most popular pet in both the United States and Great Britain. We hold our pet cats in high regard and spend billions on their food, accessory products and health care.

In contrast, the feral and stray cat population is considered by some people, and even some humane organizations, as vermin to be destroyed. Millions of cats have good homes, but even more millions of cats are feral or stray, trying to eke out a living on garbage or the kindness of a caretaker.

One thing that is evident is, regardless of their origins, the domestic cat is highly adaptable to a wide range of circumstances. They exist in almost all places in the world today, indoors and out.

Today's feral and stray cats are most likely a product of the Egyptian cat, with some interbreeding with local wild cats in the past, and very little if any purebred genetic material. Seldom do purebred cats enter the feral and stray cat gene pool because they are usually kept exclusively indoors.

Feral and stray cats in general have a wide variety of colors and color patterns, with coats that are short to medium. The cats may look similar in any one given local area due to mating of related cats or all the queens being mated to the same tomcat.

> *In my neighborhood, we have a large number of gray tabbies. This may not be that unusual except that the tabbies all have short-medium to medium coat length and every one of them has a fluffy tail. I am convinced that one fluffy-tailed tomcat is very popular.*

Domestic cats have lived successfully as both pets and feral for thousands of years. They have a proven ability to adapt to circumstance.

Is the Domestic Cat Domesticated?

There is still a controversy today whether the domestic cat is really domesticated. We can keep them happily totally indoors which would define them as domesticated. They can be feral if abandoned or born in the wild, which would classify them as wild. This duality of the cat is part of what makes it such a fascinating and lovable species.

Just because feral or stray cats can somehow scratch out a meager livelihood for themselves does not mean they should have to do it, any more than you or I. Domesticated or not, the domestic cat needs and deserves our help.

What is the Difference Between a Stray and a Feral Cat?

A tired looking underfed cat wanders into your yard or is looking for food in your trash can. You feel sorry for the poor half-starved creature and think about feeding it. Who wouldn't, except for the most heartless?

But, just as with anything else in life, there are consequences to your decision. If you don't feed the cat, it may starve or get sick in its weakened condition. If you do feed it, it will probably breed, and there will be even more underfed unwanted cats in the world, and certainly more in your neighborhood.

That's what this book is all about—helping you decide what to do to help in the most humane way possible.

There are different possibilities for the stray and feral cat. This book is directed more toward feral cats.

And just to make meanings clear, here are the definitions of the feral cat and the stray cat, for our purposes, anyway.

The Feral Cat

A feral cat is one who was born in the wild and has never been tamed. The "wild" includes the alleys, backyards, and vacant lots of cities and suburbs, as well as rural areas. The cat is not socialized to humans. A feral cat may also be a cat that was abandoned, and has not had positive experiences with humans since being abandoned. The cat has been wild so long that she or he is no longer tame.

You will not be able to get close to a feral cat. The cat may run away at the mere sight of a human.

Kittens born of feral cats are feral as well. They learn from their mothers to be afraid of humans, and just about anything else. Feral cats seem to be wary and afraid of many things. They are characteristically shy and elusive.

Feral cats are happier in the wild and are never really happy being confined. Sometimes they have to be confined if they have medical problems and need regular medication. But most of us as individuals do not have the expertise or money to care for a feral cat that has medical problems, and may be almost impossible to medicate.

Feral cats look like household domestic cats. Feral cats may be thin when you first see them, but otherwise look no different from ordinary housecats. With care and feeding, the feral cat can live a happy, healthy and free life outdoors.

The Stray Cat

A stray cat is an abandoned cat that is somewhat socialized to humans. If a cat allows you to pet her or him and seems tame, the cat is probably a stray. The cat had a home and received food and some care, but was abandoned by his or her owners or got lost. Not that it really matters. Somehow, the cat has wound up as a stray without a home or food.

If the cat can be petted, it may be adoptable. It can be adopted into an indoors only home, or an indoor and outdoor home. Being adoptable does not necessarily mean that the cat should be adopted. You may decide it is better for the cat to be treated as a feral cat.

Deciding if a Cat is Feral or Stray

Determining if a cat is feral or stray is not always clear. You will have to use your judgment for each cat. The key is: can the cat successfully adjust to a home or is it happier in the wild? If it can be adopted, is there a home available?

You may have trouble deciding whether a cat is a feral or a stray. There are many degrees of wildness. A cat may let you pet her, but that does not mean she is suitable as a house pet. Once a cat has been in the wild long enough to prefer her freedom, she is by our definition feral. Such a cat will never be happy indoors, and it is my belief that she is better left in the wild and that efforts to bring the cat indoors will not make the cat any happier.

Pearl, a cat lover, caught a feral cat and brought the cat into her apartment to tame and later put up for adoption. The cat was unable to adjust to her new surroundings. She hid out in the bedroom for two years, spending most of her time under the bed. She did finally come out of the bedroom, but never truly adjusted to life as an indoor cat. For this feral, life would have been better if she was left in her outdoor environment.

If fed properly, a feral cat can look quite well groomed and well taken care of. I have several in my yard that prove the point! But the feral cat is not a house pet, any more than a raccoon or possum. The cat can be tamed with much patience and love, but, like any wild animal, is happier in the wild (although the cat's wilderness may be your backyard or a dumpster in an alley).

For purposes of this book, a cat is feral if you believe the cat cannot or should not be adopted. This could be because:

- The cat seems wild and won't let you touch it

- You do not have a place to put the cat to socialize it

- You have other indoor cats already and cannot add more without stressing all the cats by overcrowding them

- You do not have the time or patience to socialize the cat

🐈 The cat stands little chance of being adopted and would likely have to be euthanized if a home could not be found

Feral kittens can be tamed more easily than adults and taming methods will be discussed in a later chapter.

Should You Keep a Stray or Feral Cat?

The feral or stray cat can be an ideal pet for many people. Some reasons why you may decide to keep a feral cat as an outdoor only pet:

🐈 You already have too many cats in your house (cats are so lovable that it's easy to acquire too many)

🐈 A hungry cat comes around and adopts you

🐈 You are allergic to cats and cannot have them in the house

🐈 Your rental agreement may not allow you any pets

Before deciding to keep a feral cat or cats, be sure you are committed to:

🐈 Trapping and spaying or neutering the cat(s)

🐈 Feeding regularly for an extended period

Just to make it clear, I believe it is better to keep pet cats indoors only. They are much safer indoors where there is no danger of getting run over, or getting into fights with other cats.

But we have a tremendous explosion in the cat population every spring. Kittens are born, and there are never enough homes to go around. If the kittens are taken to the average shelter, they are killed. If the kittens or cats are feral, the average shelter will not take them or they will be immediately euthanized. Because of the number of animals they take in, they must decide which are the most adoptable. Feral cats are considered unadoptable and routinely put to death without a chance at adoption. This includes young feral kittens. Even though they can be socialized if under eight weeks old, shelters do not have the time or personnel to spend socializing kittens.

Now that we know, for the purposes of this book, what we are talking about when we refer to feral and stray cats, let's talk about how you can understand a little more about them.

Cats spend most of their time sleeping.

Understanding the Stray and Feral Cat

Feral and stray cats live in the shadows of our cities and suburbs. This makes them harder to understand than our pets that we can watch and interact with. Of course, they are similar to our housecats in their reactions, all being of the same species. However, there are differences due to lifestyle.

Cats are designed to be the ultimate predator. Everything about them is designed to hunt and kill prey. Cats, being hunters, conserve energy when it is not needed. They spend as much as 18 hours a day sleeping. They avoid overexertion and overheating—they have only a very few sweat glands and cannot cool down by sweating. They hunt in short bursts of speed, not in long, tiring chases.

The feral or stray cat may be leaner and hungrier than the housecat. It will probably not have been vaccinated against disease (or may have been one time if a stray, or trapped to be spayed or neutered).

The feral or stray cat needs more food per pound of body weight than your housecat. It is more active and needs more energy to keep warm, especially in the winter.

They may have a thicker coat in the winter due to being constantly outdoors in the cold, and most likely have fleas and worms. However, having fleas and worms does not mean they cannot succeed in life, any more than other wild animals.

Their reactions are quicker and they are more cautious than housecats. They live in a hazardous environment and, like any wild animal, they must react quickly to threats to survive.

Fear of Humans

The feral cats' reactions and fear of us who feed them may be the hardest trait for us to understand. We expect them to trust us, their caretakers, since we feed them day after day, and we know we only want to help them. But our reality is much different than theirs. Most of us have medical insurance, a family, usually a steady job as a support system, and the belief that the government will help us if all of the above fails. Feral cats have none of these. They depend on themselves and, if we feed them, on us.

It is hard, if not impossible, to put ourselves in their place. Our whole lives have been spent in comparative comfort, security and ease. Their lives must seem to them like a war zone would to us—danger everywhere, lurking behind every corner and in every shadow.

They trust us only enough to come out and allow us to feed them.

In some ways, the behavior of cats in a multi-cat household resembles feral cat behavior. They react in similar ways. They adjust, make friends, or stay away from other cats. They adjust to reduced territory when a new cat enters the household. While in the house, they act more like kittens. If they go outdoors, they act more like adult cats.

Cats that have been together for a few months in the same general territory have somehow defined their relationship to the other cats. Every year there will probably be at least one new cat in the neighborhood, or new kittens appear. Some disappear as well.

Cats are a successful species, which is one reason we have the problem of too many feral and stray cats. They are adaptable. They are one of the most successful predators, yet can adapt to eating refuse in the city, or being fed by humans in the suburbs. They continue to exist in rural areas as well.

Cats are Territorial

Cats are territorial. This means that each cat has a defined territory that she hunts in and protects from other cats. Cats are attached to place, and find it very hard to be transplanted from one area to another. They hunt solitarily and the queens (adult female cats) raise the kittens by themselves without the help of the toms (adult male cats). Cats are independent creatures.

Being territorial and independent does not mean that cats are not affectionate. Nor does it excuse the abandonment of cats when people move. Cats can adjust to a new environment, and cats do form relationships with people, other cats and even other animals.

The cat is more territorial than the dog. The dog is a pack animal that lives and hunts with other dogs. The canine social structure is more defined than feline because of the close interaction of the pack. Cats definitely behave differently than dogs, and both have a different way of looking at the world than people do. I believe a lot of our misunderstanding of animals and their motives is that we expect them to think as we do.

How Large is the Feral Cat's Territory?

The size of the territory depends mainly on the food source. In the country, a cat may need as much as 25 acres to hunt if that is his sole source of food. An indoor housecat may be happy in a one-bedroom apartment, and I know of more than one person who has several indoor cats in a small apartment. According to Roger Tabor, animal behaviorist and author of *The Wild Life of the Domestic Cat*, male cats have a territory about ten times larger than females. Spayed and neutered cats need a smaller territory than intact cats.

Female cats tend to stay together and form colonies more so than males. A female cat in the suburbs may find one backyard a large enough territory.

Territories can change due to one cat being stronger than another, or a new aggressive cat moving into the territory. A change in the food supply, a cat caretaker moving and feeding stops, or someone moving in to the territory who starts feeding the cats can all change territory boundaries. The ultimate determiner of territory is the amount of food available.

Marking Territory

Territory to be defined must be marked, for the sake of the marking cat as well as other cats. Cats know they are in their territory by smelling their own scent and seeing their claw markings on objects. Marking must be done regularly for the cats to feel secure in their territory. All cats mark, both male and female.

One way cats like to mark is by scratching upright objects such as trees and wooden fence posts. This is done by clawing the object. Other cats can detect the claw marks and the scent of the marks. Cats can tell much about other cats by the markings they leave. We do not always easily notice the markings. However, when our housecat claws his or her territory (our furniture) in the house, we do notice this quite easily, and perhaps somewhat emotionally.

Another method of marking is by urine spraying on upright objects. We notice this odor quite easily, and we can become quite upset when we smell it in our home. The unaltered males tend to do this more than other cats, and their odor is the most pungent. Housecats often do not spray urine unless under stress, usually when a new cat is brought into their "territory." It is natural for all cats to want to mark their territory.

Face Rubbing

Face rubbing is also a form of marking. Cats have glands on the sides of their faces that give off a scent that is undetectable to humans but cats can smell. That is why your cat rubs her head against you; she is marking you as part of her clan. It is a sign of ownership and affection. Cats also rub their heads against objects to show ownership and that the object is part of their territory.

Head Butting

Head butting is a sign of affection and is usually done only to other cats and people, not objects. This is done by slightly dipping down and then hopping up to butt the head against a hand of a human or under the head of another cat. Affectionate cats may spend a lot of time head rubbing and butting.

Feral and stray cats spend much of their time alone, but they do form what I call friendships. They then rub their heads against each other to show affection. Sometimes two cats will circle around each while rubbing and head bumping.

Fecal Marking

We usually think of cats as a being neat and clean since they use the litterbox and carefully bury their feces. However, in the wild, burying their feces may be a sign of subordination. According to Roger Tabor, animal behaviorist, most feral cats bury their feces, while dominant cats leave theirs uncovered, sometimes in prominent positions. Feral cats often bury their feces at the far edges of their territory, so it is likely that it is a form of territory marking.

Hunting

The cat hunts her prey alone. This makes for a whole different style of behavior than the dog that hunts in a pack. The cat is much more cautious with her prey than the pack hunting dog, taking care not to get bitten. Having only herself to depend upon for food, the cat must be careful not to get injured. This accounts for the fact of cat "playfulness" with her prey. The cat may actually be wearing the catch down so that the cat will not be bitten. Bites can become infected easily and, with no one to bring food back to her or her kittens, she must be cautious about injury.

Cats seem to be able to hunt instinctually, although having a mother cat that shows her kittens how to hunt increases their hunting ability. However, the hunting instinct does not make the average feral city or suburban cat an accomplished hunter capable of feeding herself. The density of the feral cat population in most areas means there is not enough prey to hunt to keep the feral cat population alive and healthy. Most feral or semi-feral cats survive with human help either by people feeding the cats directly or the cats scavenging from human garbage.

If the mother cat hunts, she will start teaching her kittens to hunt at about five to six weeks of age. She will start by bringing them food, and may bring back stunned prey to teach the kittens how to kill. The kittens will naturally hunt insects and pounce on moving things, as well as stalk "prey." However, if the mother does not teach the kittens how to kill, they may only know how to hunt and "play" with their prey, never learning to kill.

Birds as Prey

There is concern by some people and organizations about feral and stray cats contributing to the loss of the bird population. Most cats do not catch many birds. The cat is best suited to catching rodents. Mice are the cat's preferred prey.

From personal experience in my years of cat feeding, there was only one cat that ever caught any prey, and in a period of about two years, I only saw two birds he caught and ate. According to Desmond Morris in his book, *Cat Watching*, "the excellent eyesight of birds and their ability to fly straight up in the air to escape make them unsuitable targets for domestic cats." The main contributor to bird declining numbers is humanity. We are spreading out into previously wild places, leaving less and less space for wildlife. Wildlife, including birds, needs more undisturbed territory. Biologist Dr. Robert Berg states, "As man's development of the planet continues, available habitat for animals and plants is being carved up into smaller pieces."

Again, most city and suburban stray and feral cats rely on what humans give them or what they get out of trash bins.

Cats are true carnivores, designed to eat mostly meat, but make effective scavengers if that is what they must do to survive.

When I first brought in a semi-feral cat, Ernie (later discovered to have a mistaken identity; Ernie is female—but that is another story), who was about six months old, she would try to eat my leftovers or any food left on a counter. After a few years, she lost her scavenger instinct and would only eat her favorite name brand cat food and an occasional treat of Colonel Sanders' Kentucky Fried Chicken. She has a real craving for the chicken.

How Cats Experience the World

Cats experience the world very differently than we do. Their senses are more highly developed than ours. Cats see better than us, especially in the dark, however they give up some of their color perception for better night vision. Cats' hearing and sense of smell are more acute than humans. Because of their sensitivity and their timid natures, loud or sudden noises, as well as quick or sudden movements can easily startle cats. When startled, their natural instinct is to run and hide.

Being solitary hunters encourages a fear of injury, which increases their timidity. Their heightened senses make them more sensitive to their surroundings and any change can upset them. A sound that is not disturbing to us can upset cats whose hearing is sensitive enough to hear a mouse scurrying in the grass. They can sense emotions in those around them, and timid cats are easily upset by human emotions as well as by other more aggressive cats.

Kenny and Steve are my two former feral kittens that are now indoor only cats. Steve is much more aggressive than Kenny. He has been that way since they were kittens, and they are, as of this writing, four years old. Kenny always gives in to his brother Steve. If Steve wants Kenny's food, Kenny just lets him take it. No fight, Kenny just walks away. Kenny is more sensitive than Steve, more easily startled. He runs when someone comes to the door, and rarely comes out when people visit unless they have been in the house many times. He can hide out for hours at a time after being startled. This behavior may be because his mother was a very timid feral cat, and he was not socialized early enough (they were about eight weeks old when I brought them indoors). Read more about socialization in a later chapter.

Many household cat behavior problems can be traced to cats' sensitivity to their surroundings. We need to be aware of what kinds of energy we are putting out in our environment, and try keep our home atmosphere as peaceful as possible.

Although feral cats are wild, they are not all the same in temperament. Since they are basically domesticated cats that have returned to the wild, they have the characteristics of the different cats that make up their ancestry. Some are more passive like Persians and other less active cats; some are more like the Siamese who are more active and vocal. Persians and Siamese are at opposite ends of the spectrum of cat temperament. Although the two breeds are used as an example, in actuality, most feral cats do not have purebred cat ancestry. Most purebred cats are kept indoors only, and rarely wind up as strays. Stray and feral cats are probably more like their wild ancestors than any purebred cat.

Because of their lifestyle, and the fact they are probably very much like their original wild cat ancestors, most feral cats live a fairly active life. Feral cats, if startled, can leave an area in seconds.

Some feral cats are so shy you may never see them. There are some cats that eat the food I put out only after I go back into the house. I see these "shadow" cats only occasionally through the window, and sometimes when they are especially hungry or brave at the edge of the yard or on the fence. Others cats, although feral, seem more confident, and want to be petted after a period of time (but be aware that the "period of time" may run to years).

Feral cats do not necessarily trust you even if you feed them every day for years. They do not seem to relate the fact of your setting food out for them every day with safety, or perhaps they just cannot trust any human. I guess this is like children who do not receive love when young, and then can never accept that they are loved no matter how anyone shows it to them later in life. Sometimes background and/or experiences cannot be overcome. Some experts believe that if kittens are not socialized before four months of age, they can never be truly socialized. The cats can never let us know what they have been through, so part of their background is always a mystery.

Some cats will eventually let you get closer as time goes on, but I am not convinced that such cats can ever be good pets or, more importantly, would be happy being a pet. Timid feral cats may be as happy as possible living in their familiar territory.

Cat Stress

What stresses cats most is change. They like to eat the same food and stay in the same territory. In this way, feral and stray cats are no different than housecats. They are happier staying in the place they are born, in the same territory, eating the same food at the same time everyday.

Sometimes well-meaning people try to tame feral cats so they can give them a good home. Although the motivation is admirable, if a cat is really feral, timid, and distrustful of people, this may not be a blessing. After a cat has been free, the cat most probably has no desire to be shut in a house. The cat may feel trapped and mourn the loss of her or his freedom.

This is a judgment issue. Before deciding whether to bring a feral cat inside to be socialized, you must decide if the cat will truly be happier.

People report cats hiding under beds for years before becoming socialized. I do not believe this is in the best interest of the cat. Again, if we remember these cats are wild animals, it helps us to make the best decision. Would you bring the same animal in the house if it was a raccoon or squirrel? Probably not. It is easier to understand that a raccoon or squirrel is a wild animal that is happiest living outdoors because we rarely see them as pets.

But of course, the lines between a feral and stray cat are not always clear. The cat may let you stroke her, and even pick her up. Does this mean the cat belongs indoors? Maybe. But keep in mind that cats do not like change, even what you may believe is a change for the better.

Feral Cat Social Life

Feral cat social structure is more loosely defined than either human or dog. They do not have much of a hierarchal structure. They, being solitary hunters, have no need for a pack or leader of the pack, so they deal with each other as equals. This does not mean that one cat does not protect his territory or food from another cat. When fed as a group, one cat or two cats will usually eat first and others will wait until those cats are finished before eating. So there is a form of hierarchy in a group situation. However, this would not necessarily happen in nature without human interference.

Buck and Cher with Spot in background

Cats do form relationships. I have found that after being spayed or neutered some form what I call friendships. They lie together or near each other at times, and walk closely together.

> *Cher is the exquisite crème colored, blue-eyed mother of Steve and Kenny, two of my indoor only cats. Cher (who was trapped and spayed) has formed a friendship with Buck, a gray tabby male that looks much like a Maine Coon cat with his thick coat and ruff around his neck. They often sleep together in the backyard, which is the center of their territory. They walk side by side with their tails entwined around each other at the tip, much as humans might walk hand in hand. I think Buck watches out for Cher. She is so timid that she will not eat if another cat even looks at her oddly. I often wonder how she survived long enough to have Steve and Kenny, my two formerly feral kittens.*

Relationships are most easily formed between littermates whether the cats are indoors or out.

Spike and Spot, two of the very shy kittens from a feral mother, come around for food although the mother and her two other offspring do not. Spike, a neutered male, and Spot, a spayed female, have been fed for three years, but still always stay at the far end of the yard until I go back into the house. They may someday allow me to pet them, but they will never be pet material. Cats from the same litter seem to get along best, but friendships can form as in the example of Cher and Buck.

Cher, Buck, Spike and Spot all live outdoors and are healthy and well fed and appear to enjoy life. They can be spotted from time to time in a favorite sunning spot or just relaxing on the top of the fence.

Buck relaxing on the fence.

Feeding Time

Cat behavior at feeding time shows a kind of structure. Some cats always eat first, some always last.

> Cher, Steve and Kenny's mother, always waits for all the other cats to eat before she does. A cat has only to look at her and she will shy away from the food. It has been this way since she was a kitten with her littermates. I was feeding the four kittens every day. Then an aggressive and hungry cat came around. He chased all four of them away. At first I shooed the new cat away and watched over the kittens until they had enough. But as soon as I left the yard, he would chase them away and start eating.
>
> I realized, after a few weeks of this routine, with no change in the behavior of the cats, that I had to let them work this out for themselves.
>
> The aggressive cat kept chasing them away. But eventually Cher returned (the others did not) after giving birth to Steve and Kenny. For some reason, the aggressive cat took a liking to her, let her eat, eventually made friends with her and even protected her from other cats.

It is not necessarily the most aggressive cat that eats first. Cats seldom fight over food if there is enough, which is the case most times when being fed by a caretaker. Mother cats with growing kittens can be pretty aggressive about feeding. If all the cats are spayed or neutered, there is very little fighting. Once in a while, they make a clawing movement at each other or hiss, but no one is actually hurt. If feeding is regular and enough food is there, all the cats will eat, but all may not eat at once.

Some cats show up at the regular feeding time and others, mainly tomcats, show up later. The tomcats seem to be making their regular rounds of different locations in their larger territories. They may have another regular source of food, and just stroll by for an occasional dessert.

Cat Communication

Some people believe that animals do not communicate because they do not use words. Animals communicate differently, with gestures, eye movements, and sounds. Their communication may not be as detailed and intricate as ours, but they definitely do communicate.

Feral and stray cat communication is much quieter than our housecats. Our pet cats learn to be more verbal because they learn we understand verbal communication better than cat gestures and signs. Feral cats that you feed can learn to be more verbal.

> *Spot, although she will not let me get closer than 10 or 12 feet from her, will meow loudly when I come out with the food. Her meow sounds like she is saying, "Hurry up, I'm really hungry."*

The cat uses facial expressions and ears to communicate. In a happy, untroubled mood, a cat's ears will face forward. If alert, the eyes will be open, if sleepy, the eyes will be half closed or barely open.

An irritated cat will move her ears to the side, the eyes will have a more slit-eyed shape, the tail will switch, and she may growl. A cat that is expecting or starting a fight will have the ears back, head lowered and stare directly at the rival cat.

Do not stare directly at a feral cat. Cats find a direct stare intimidating, and will usually leave if you keep your eyes on them. Instead, try to observe them while seeming to look at or doing something else.

Fighting

Most cat fights are between male cats, but because of the cat's territorial nature, fights between male and female cats do occur. However, most serious battles are between two males. Cat fights, although rare amongst neutered males, can cause problems for feral cats.

Cat fights are where most serious injuries occur with the exception of road accidents. It is also the situation where cat diseases are transferred. Cat scratches are transmitters of disease and scratches are also easily infected.

Fighting and mating are the two times when cats make the most noise. The loud, menacing sounds the cats make before the fight and during mating are hard to ignore. The noise itself is a problem for the city/suburban feral cat. Neighbors may object to having these loud cat utterances disturbing their sleep.

Feral Cat Sex

This is the main reason for fighting between unaltered males, which is usually late at night and noisy. Cats' mating is also noisy, and disturbing to the neighbors as well.

You do not need to know much about feral cat sex except:

🐾 You want to avoid this (sex) happening and bringing more unwanted (by the human population) kittens into the world.

🐾 This is the major public relations problem for your feral cats.

Cat mating and fighting are also the main causes of spreading two of the most deadly cat diseases, FelV and FIV (FelV is also transmitted by social contact such as mutual grooming). These two diseases are spread through bites and scratches which happen mainly during sex and cat fights, both of which rarely occur amongst spayed and neutered cats that have enough to eat. A female cat will mate with more than one male cat, and this increases the chance for spreading of disease.

I have read reports that FIV is not common amongst feral and stray cats. However, I trapped two adult male cats that had severe bites. Both cats were positive for FIV.

One eight-week-old kitten that I trapped I had tested for FIV. I do not usually do this since I do not want to have to make the decision to euthanize the cat if he or she is positive. But the kitten was young and had to have the test before he could be adopted. He was positive. FIV can be contracted by kittens from their mothers.

This experience made me more determined to spay and neuter the cats in the neighborhood since having sex can be a death sentence for these cats.

This chapter is not a complete discussion of cat behavior. It is just a brief introduction with the emphasis on feral cats. For more information on feral cat behavior, see the appendix.

Now that you have more of an understanding of the feral cat you have seen in your yard, trash or wherever you have noticed it, what do you do next?

Care of the Feral or Stray Cat

*W*e live in an overcrowded world: too many people, and too many unwanted pets. You want to help the stray or feral cat at your door, yet you don't want to be part of the problem of bringing more stray and feral cats into the world.

According to the Feral Cat Coalition of San Diego, California, "A pair of breeding cats, which can have two or more litters per year, can exponentially produce 420,000 offspring over a seven-year period." I believe this number assumes that all the kittens survive. Feral kittens don't have all the advantages of pets. The mother cat may not have had any immunization shots and not have any immunities to pass on to the kittens. There may not be enough food, and what is found by the mother may not be the most nutritious.

Keeping the overabundance of feral cats in mind, the two most important points in managing your feral cats are:

1. Feed regularly and do not put out more food than the cats can finish within one to two hours.

Adjust amounts as needed. For instance, a mother cat may join your group. You will trap and have her spayed, but you are not in the business of destroying lives but saving them. She will need more food while she is nursing her kittens. The kittens, in turn, will either join the group or, if tame enough, be put up for adoption. They will also be spayed and neutered.

2. Spay and neuter any cats that enter your group.

This is the primary method to keep the cat population down without killing. This is the most humane thing you can do for the cats.

You need to remind yourself from time to time that you can help, but you (or any other one individual) cannot do it all for feral and stray cats. You cannot help all the cats, but you can make a big difference for the ones you do help. You need to be able to care for the feral cats properly, and this means a good diet for them, money for spaying and neutering, shots, and medical care if needed, and if you can catch the cats.

Feral or stray cats do not require the financial outlay of pets, as you may not be able to get the cats to the veterinarian for vaccinations and medical care. Trapping more than once is not easy, as the cats get trap wise, so most of the time, medical care is only on an emergency basis when the cat is too sick to fight or run from you. Oftentimes, that will be too late to help, but that is the reality.

Time

Another factor is time. It does not take much time to set food and water out for the cats, but occasionally you will have to trap a cat, take the cat to the vet to get spayed or neutered, or a cat may need medical help. You also may have sick or orphan kittens that you decide to hand raise.

Space

Space is another issue. If there are too many cats in an area, cats get stressed and may fight or have other behavior that is a problem for the cats, you, and/or others in your neighborhood.

Neighbors

Even if you have the money and the time, if you are feeding too many cats your neighbors may be concerned. Cats really have very little protection under our legal system, especially feral and stray cats. They can be trapped and killed with no protection from the law. It is not to the cats' advantage to be seen as a problem by your neighbors.

You cannot save all the feral cats. It may be best to keep a rather low profile about the cats in your neighborhood. If people know you are sympathetic to cats, they may decide to dump, literally, their problems on you.

Setting Limits

When it comes to managing your feral and stray cats, you need to set limits. Decide how much you can afford in time and money. Then stick to your plan. I know this can be difficult when yet another adorable cat or kitten shows up at your door. If you are diligent about spaying and neutering, you should not have a problem with extra cats. But you may have a neighbor who gets a

cute kitten every year, and just stops feeding it when he or she gets tired of the kitten as he or she grows bigger.

The cute kitten is then a stray, and since it will probably not be spayed or neutered by such an owner, may turn up in your yard pregnant or as a tom that is fighting with your other cats.

It was Cher's mother with her kittens that first got me interested in the plight of feral cats. This emaciated mother and her four kittens (including Cher) showed up walking along the concrete block wall on the far end of my tiny backyard. I watched her and her scrawny kittens for a few days, thinking about the consequences if I did feed them: other cats may come around; raccoons, skunks, and possums could come around if I put food out. This could create even more problems for me than I was solving for the mother and kittens. After a few days of thinking, I remembered reading somewhere that starving to death was one of the cruelest ways to die. I decided to feed them and accept the consequences. That first bag of cat food I bought for that mother cat and kittens changed my life.

What are the consequences of feeding the mother cat and kittens or the tom that comes around?

What You Need to Know Before You Start Feeding

If you feed a feral cat without spaying or neutering her or him, you *will* be part of the problem. The female cat you feed will reproduce at least once, and maybe twice, a year. The tomcat can be the father of many litters. The kittens will be cute although wild. What will you do with them? Your feral cat population can swell immensely in a short amount of time.

Your local shelter or humane society probably will not be of much help for the feral cats. The main function of most humane societies is to control the animal population, which translates to keeping the population down. They do their best to find homes for cats, but most shelters have far too many tame cats and kittens to place and are forced to euthanize many of the tame cats and kittens placed in their care. Shelters are set up to keep animals for only a short period of time. Because of the many animals turned in to shelters, they must make room for new animals on a daily basis. Animals that are not considered adoptable because of age, health, or temperament may be euthanized immediately to make way for adoptable animals. There are very few no kill shelters at this time.

Most shelters will not take feral cats since they are not readily adoptable and they do not have a program to house and feed them. They do not have enough personnel or space to keep feral cats for the time it takes to tame them, assuming the cat is considered tamable. For the most part, shelters cannot help feral cats. They routinely euthanize them. Only individual people and the few organizations set up to assist feral cats can help.

Resources

Resources refer to both time and money. Although it doesn't take much time to set food out once or twice a day, it does take some time to trap the cats and take them to and from the vet. And it does take money, although there are organizations that will help you pay for spaying and neutering. See the appendix for some of them.

Other Ways to Help Feral Cats

If you feel you do not have the resources to help feral cats on your own but still want to help, consider contributing time or money to an organization dedicated to helping feral cats. Organizations who help feral cats are listed in the appendix. These organizations offer help when you have feral cat challenges. Some have members you can telephone for advice, and/or Internet bulletin boards dedicated to questions and answers about feral cats.

Spay and Neuter

You can make sure your own pets are spayed and neutered, and encourage others about spaying and neutering their pets. Many people think letting the kids see birth is educational, and don't think ahead about what to do with the kittens after they are weaned. This kind of learning does not train children to value life. Such lessons teach children that a "scientific" experiment is more important than the consequences for the victims of the experiment. The scientific method teaches to suppress emotions and do what is necessary to prove or disprove a theory. This kind of thinking is okay up to a point, but when the experiments include animals whose rights and feelings are disregarded, I think we need to modify our idea of scientific thinking. Some feeling and compassion needs to be included in the scientific ideal.

> *I was shopping in a large discount store, when a man seeing me in the cat aisle, started talking to me about the cat his son had left with him when he moved out. He said the cat did not need to be neutered since he was a male and would not have any kittens. I told him how neutering him would keep the cat from spraying in the house, and reduce his wandering. I also told him about the prevalence of FIV and how it was spread by fighting, and that there were organizations that would help with the cost if that was a problem. He said he hadn't known the facts regarding neutering, and that he would take the cat to get neutered. I can only hope that he did.*

Think of consequences before taking action to help feral cats. Your responsibilities will be to:

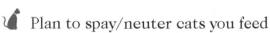 Plan to spay/neuter cats you feed

Choose food that will meet dietary needs

Have enough dishes or pans to feed all

 Set out an appropriate amount of food at each feeding

or

 Consider alternative ways to help feral cats; help other individuals who are feeding feral cats, join a humane organization devoted to feral cats, volunteer, or give money to a feral cat organization, and tell others about their responsibility to spay or neuter their pets

If we are to help, we must understand that feral cats are not pets in the usual sense, and will not get the same care that our pet housecats receive. They may not get regular vaccinations, or medical care if injured. If they do get medical care, it is usually emergency care when the cats are too ill to struggle against us or run away and hide.

I believe feral cats deserve to live their lives in freedom, and helping them responsibly can make it a better world for us as well as for them. It is not until we treat all life as valuable and with respect that we can fully reach our potential as human beings.

Feeding

*W*hen you first see a feral or stray cat it is probably because the cat is hungry. The cat may be in good condition or pitifully thin. Whichever is the case, before you feed the cat make sure it is feral or stray and does not belong to someone else. The cat is probably feral or stray:

🐈 If she will not let you near her. Sometimes, though, the cat may have had some positive human contact and may let you get close or even touch her. In that case, you may want to ask the neighbors if the cat is theirs.

🐈 If she is friendly and lets you pet her and comes up and begs for food, she may be a stray, but you should still check with the neighbors. In that case, you have a decision to eventually make. Is the cat a stray that can be adopted or is she feral and happier left as she is?

After you are sure the cat is feral or stray and not owned by someone else, you need to feed and water him or her first thing. A cat that is hungry will eat lots of things your fussy housecat may not. They survive on garbage, leftovers, and rodents. Most feral cats in cities and suburbs are scavengers. If not fed regularly by someone, their main food supply is garbage and leftovers.

This may surprise some owners of cats that are fussy eaters. The fussy cat may just be stubbornly holding out for what he or she wants and trying to "train" the owner to provide the food desired.

Be Prepared

Before you start feeding, make sure you have the resources to trap, spay and neuter as well as feed the cat(s). If you do not, think twice before feeding. If you don't have enough money to spay and neuter, you will soon not have enough money to feed, because there will be so many cats! As cruel as it may seem, it may be better to let nature take its course (not that this is advised by the author).

You need to make sure you have enough money to feed the cats a decent diet. A low quality pet food might seem okay when compared to what the cats might otherwise scavenge to eat, but if the cats are not nourished properly, they most likely will become ill. Decide what you can afford from the beginning since cats fed canned food may not want to change to dry food. Remember, cats do not like change.

What to Feed

What I suggest you feed your feral kitties is a recognized brand of cat food that states that it is nutritionally complete such as Friskies, Purina, or

Whiskas, or the premium brands such as Hills or Iams. You can get either dry or canned food, depending on your budget and preference. By buying name national brands, you know that the food has been tested and proved to be a balanced diet that maintains health in cats. If you get the store brand or an off brand, you do not have this assurance. Some store or off brands are nutritionally balanced and some are not, and you have no way of knowing which ones are adequate. Also, the ingredients may be less desirable in a cheaper brand, or have a larger percentage of fillers.

I feed my feral cats a major brand of dry food found in the supermarket. My indoor cats (all either former feral or stray) get the same dry food and a small amount of canned food each day. Both the feral cats and the indoor pets are healthy and sleek with shiny coats. Since I feed five to six or more feral cats every day (I have six regulars, as of today, and others that show up sometimes or wait until I leave to eat) I buy the 18 or 20 lb bags of dry food. This is more convenient (less trips to the store) and less expensive than buying smaller bags. Sometimes in my area it is hard to find the larger sizes of the brand of food I buy in the grocery store. I have found that I can get the larger sizes and the varieties I want by buying the food on the internet at the online pet stores. The prices online are good, as of today, but be careful when buying food online or through catalogs to check the delivery charge. Delivery charges have been reasonable, but appear to be going up. The advantage to ordering online is it saves lugging the bags home.

Don't feed the really cheap foods. They will not keep your colony of cats in good shape. Only the major companies have the resources to do studies to make sure the food they sell is nutritionally complete. Assume that the cats cannot get other food, and plan for them to have a balanced diet on strictly what you are feeding them. Dry is fine as long as it is a major brand that says nutritionally complete on the label.

One advantage of dry food is that it does last a while when set outside without getting flies all over it in hot weather, or dried up and inedible. I feed the feral kitties in the morning enough food so that every cat that is out there is fed, and there is a little left over if a cat comes by later. It is always gone after about two hours, or when I come home from work in the evening. Leaving out more than they can eat in an hour or two is not good. It encourages other animals that you do not want and insects to come around.

Kittens should have kitten food if possible, especially if trapped or caught and are no longer getting their mother's milk. Again, a major brand kitten food is fine. However, if they are feral kittens still with their mother, you are feeding several cats and cannot afford the kitten food, the adult food will be okay. Feral cat mothers do not usually wean their kittens until three to four months of age, so it is likely that the kittens will be eating and receiving nourishment from their mother as well. If you can afford it, you could put out kitten food for a few weeks. The problem is you usually have to put it out for all the cats since you cannot control which cat eats which food.

When to Feed

Try to feed and water the cats about the same time(s) every day. Cats like regularity. They soon begin to know when it is feeding time. The cats I feed sit by the backdoor and wait for me at feeding time, or actually, anytime they think it should be feeding time. They know what time the food comes, and sometimes look longingly in the window at me. That does not mean I can pet them or even get near them when I go outside.

Feeding at a regular time is important. I feed all the cats, indoors and outdoors, in the morning, because this is the only time I can feed at a regular time with certainty. I am never sure when I will get home from work, errands, etc., so this is the best time to keep them on a regular schedule. Choose the best time you can feed them regularly and conveniently. The key is regularity, whether your cats are feral or not. Regularity gives the cats a feeling of security, knowing they will be fed. I believe this also keeps the fighting down. They know they will be fed, and there is enough food for all. Sometimes it takes awhile for new cats to your group to understand this and fit in without upsetting the other cats.

I only put out in the morning what will be gone in a few hours. This is dry food. It would be even more important for wet food. Flies and ants get in the food if left out for too long, and cats will not eat food with ants in it. I don't believe you can leave a constant food source out for outdoor cats. It is just too attractive to other animals and insects.

If food is leftover, soon you will find you have other animals coming around. Skunks and raccoons are nocturnal and like cat food. They may decide to hang out around a regular food supply. I don't know about you, but I don't particularly like skunks around my house. You can smell them and they seem to enjoy nesting under the house.

If food is left over after two hours, start cutting down on the amount fed. There should be nothing left. If you think the cats need more food, add more gradually. If you leave too much food out, you will attract more and more cats as well as the other animals in your neighborhood. This is okay, as long as you can afford to feed them and you do not have too many cats that are seen as a nuisance by your neighbors. Only so many cats can be in a given territory without it becoming overcrowded. If overcrowded, you have other problems to deal with in addition to the cats.

I repeat, do NOT leave out more food than the cats eat in an hour or two, especially in the evening. The most common wild animals that might start eating the cat food are nocturnal. If these animals become pests, the usual way to eliminate them is to kill them. You do not want to have to do that, so it is best not to encourage them to be around the area in the first place.

Dogs can also be a problem. The food must be protected from them. I put the food in my fenced backyard and have the gate closed.

When I first began feeding the feral kitties, there were three large dogs that roamed free in the neighborhood. I fed all the cats before I left for work, and all the food was gone when I got home. One Saturday I heard a load noise and looked out the window to the backyard. One of the large dogs bounded into the yard. The cats all ran and jumped over the fence. The dog then proceeded to wolf down all the food in the dish in less than one minute. After that, I kept the gate locked to make sure the dogs couldn't get in.

The food must be put where dogs cannot get it. Or you can wait outside until the cats eat to make sure no dogs come around until the cats have their fill. In that situation, as a precaution I suggest you pick up the food after they have eaten so there is no attractive nuisance for dogs or other animals.

Another problem where I live is ants. If food is left out in the summer, ants quickly come and run all over it (this includes the dry food) and then the cats will not eat it. In winter the food can freeze. Be thrifty with the food. Leave out enough but not too much. Measure the food. This should keep your feral and stray cat charges well fed and happy.

Water

Water must be available at all times, but especially if you are feeding dry food. The water should be fresh daily. This is very important, for the cats may not have access to clean water or any water at all.

Cats do not need milk. In fact, milk can sometimes cause diarrhea. I suggest that you do not give the cats milk.

Food Containers

You will need several dishes for food so they don't fight over one dish, or one cat is left without any food after the dominant cat(s) are finished. You will also need at least one large water container or several containers of water. They must have water at all times, especially if you are feeding them dry food.

Food containers should be sturdy and solid, with enough heaviness and stability to stay in one place. I find that having several smaller containers instead of one large one makes it more likely that all cats will get fed and avoid kitty aggressiveness. I also put the dishes about three feet or more away from each other so that the timid cats do not feel threatened by the more aggressive cats. Otherwise, an aggressive cat may chase away a more timid cat that then may go hungry.

I am not sure why, but some cats just seem to be more aggressive than others. Some are so timid that they will not fight for the food, and will just let any other cat eat first even if extremely hungry. There is some kind of social structure here, for the other cats just go over and eat, while the timid cat or cats wait until they are done and eat what is left. Usually there is no fight, they have just worked out a system.

Water can be in one large dish that is not easily tipped over. Cats don't seem to fight over the water, just drink a little at a time.

Heavy plastic containers with a wide base are best for the water. The food containers can also be of the same heavy plastic, but the thinner less expensive plastic dishes that do not topple over easily can be used as well. Cats seem to prefer lower, flatter dishes to eat out of, probably so they can see any danger approaching. Each cat does not need his or her own dish, although this is ideal, because some will wait until the others eat no matter how many dishes are put down, and some cats will share a dish. I would suggest having at least one dish for every three cats that show up at feeding time.

Food should be put where it can be out of the weather if possible, under some kind of roof so the food won't get in the rain or too much sun. This keeps the food in good condition for the one to two hours it may take for it to be eaten by all the cats that need feeding.

To deal with the overcrowding issue before it becomes a problem, go to the next chapter on trapping.

Remember to:

🐱 Use quality nutritionally complete food

🐱 Always have water available

🐱 Feed on a regular schedule

🐱 Use containers that are shallow and do not tip over easily

Trap, Spay or Neuter, and Release (TNR)

The trap, neuter, and release program (TNR) is the basic element of controlling your stray cat numbers. It will take you no more than a year to decide that spaying or neutering your cats is necessary. If stray and feral cats are fed without spaying or neutering them, they quickly produce kittens and their numbers will become far too many for you to handle or your neighborhood to contain. The cats will become more competitive as their territory becomes over-crowded, and unaltered cats will noisily fight for territory and mates. The noise will probably annoy the non-cat lovers in the your neighborhood, and you as well when you are awakened from a good night's sleep. Therefore, it is a good idea for you to act as the public relations representative of your strays.

Spay/neuter = less noise
Less noise = good neighbor

The TNR Program

The TNR program consists of:

- Trapping the cats in a humane animal trap that leaves the cat unharmed

- Taking the cat to the veterinarian and having him neutered or her spayed

- Returning the cat to his or her territory.

The TNR program is outlined in detail in this chapter.

This chapter is important for strays, but if you need more convincing, read the following:

Susan was feeding four or five cats that were feral. She knew about the importance of spaying and neutering. She was kind hearted and did not want to frighten the cats by trapping. She also had moral issues that led her to believe it was wrong to spay and neuter.

Things worked out fine for a year or so. Because the cats had such good care and a regular supply of food, most of the kittens survived, and had more kittens themselves.

After three years, Susan had 200 cats, more or less (she could not get an accurate count). Things were out of control, she could not feed that many cats and getting them spayed and neutered was a major undertaking. She called a rescue organization for desperately needed help. Luckily for Susan, the organization was able to help her trap, spay and neuter the cats, as well as find caretakers for some of the cats.

If the cat is a stray and you can pick her up and put her into a cat carrier to go to the veterinarian, do that. The information in this chapter is for feral cats, those you cannot get into a cat carrier. If unsure, I suggest you trap the cat.

Warning: A frightened cat can inflict painful scratches and bites that can require medical attention. It is a good idea to make sure your tetanus immunization is current.

Cat Trapping Made Easy

One of the biggest obstacles I had to overcome in my own spay and neuter program for the feral and stray cats in my neighborhood was not wanting to hurt the cats I was trapping. I felt compassion for the cats, thinking I knew how frightened the cats would be, first trapped, and then being taken to a strange place, put to sleep and wake up in pain. Even though I knew it was in the best interest of the cats, I felt uncomfortable about trapping.

My other obstacle was my belief that it was difficult to trap a cat. It's not.

Steve and Kenny, my indoor former feral kitties, were taken from their mother, Cher, when they were seven weeks old because they were sick and needed medication four times a day. After giving the two kittens medication for over one month, I decided to adopt them even though I did not want any more cats indoors. I had too much emotional investment in them.

> *Two weeks after I took the kittens from Cher and her milk had dried up, I trapped her. She was the first cat I ever trapped. It was only the realization that I could not adopt all the kittens that were born, and that next time she would probably have four kittens that gave me the resolve to overcome my reluctance to trap.*
>
> *I made trapping her much more difficult than it had to be. Because of my concern about frightening her, it took me three days to trap her.*
>
> *Cher is still a very timid cat that will not eat until all the other cats are finished. She is healthy and as happy as I believe she can be living in the outdoors.*

After I adopted Steve and Kenny, I realized that I could not adopt all the new kittens that come into the world, and that life can be hard for feral kittens. My experience with Steve and Kenny forced me to realize how important spaying and neutering is for the feral and stray cats that we care about.

Steps to Trapping

Step One: *Make sure cat(s) are ready to be spayed or neutered*

For adult cats, try to find out if the cat is already spayed or neutered. See if the cat's ear is notched or clipped to show it has been spayed or neutered.

It is generally recommended that feral cats, while still under general anesthetic for spaying or neutering, have the top quarter inch of their left ear removed by a straight cut. The shape of this ear is unmistakable, even at a distance. Properly done, ear tipping allows the caretaker to easily spot any new cat entering the colony, and neutered cats will not have to be retrapped. Any ear-tipped cat trapped in error can be identified within the trap and released. Alley Cat Allies, along with the international community, is promoting widespread publicity for ear tipping as the preferred universal method for identifying neutered feral cats belonging to controlled colonies.

If the cat seems relatively tame you may also want to check with the neighbors to see if someone owns it. The owner may have already had the cat altered. The ear notching or clipping is normally only done to feral cats. A stray may have been altered but not have the notched or clipped ear. If the cat is someone else's, which is highly unlikely if it is feral cat, you may want to make sure your trapping and altering the cat is approved by the person who claims ownership. If the owner resists, you may want to explain the consequences of having kittens who will be wild in a world where tame kittens are destroyed for lack of homes for them. If the cat is male, it is very likely he will eventually die of injuries or disease transmitted through fighting in addition to fathering the above mentioned kittens.

If the cat is female, try to find out if she has a litter that is not yet weaned somewhere. If she does, you need to wait until the litter is weaned before trapping her. It is better, if possible, to wait until the kittens are no longer nursing before trapping. But do not wait too long, or you may have another litter on your hands. Female cats can become pregnant while still nursing, and feral cat mothers often nurse the kittens even after they are eating solid food, sometimes until the kittens are three or four months old. Check with your veterinarian for each individual cat situation.

There is a spay procedure that is currently widely used in Europe but rarely utilized in the United States. This surgical technique is called the "left lateral flank spay," and involves making a small incision through the lateral abdominal wall of the cat. Basically, this technique involves going through the side of the animal as opposed to the animal's stomach area. The animal is shaved on the left flank area. Originally, this technique was developed for use on feral cats who were going to be released into the wild within 48 hours of having the surgery.

Faith Maloney, Director of Animal Care at Best Friends Animal Sanctuary in Utah, states, "Nursing, once it's in operation, is not affected by the spay. Nursing is a response to suckling and a hormone in the brain, not the reproductive system. We spay nursing mothers and return them immediately to their location. One of the vets we work with uses the flank spay method. The incision is on the flank not on the belly mid-line. The incision can be as small as the width of the scalpel, and the skin is closed with glue. This leaves the belly clear for nursing and also prevents putting strain on the stitch line if the cat jumps. Diane Young, who does our feral cat program for the local community, will spay or neuter any cat that gets into the trap, as she may never see it again!"

If the cat is male, try to see if he is intact. This may be hard if the cat has a long coat. Also, watch the cat's behavior. If the cat is fighting, he is probably intact. If he is more easy-going, he may be neutered, but the cat's behavior is not a sure sign.

Kittens can be as young as eight or nine weeks old when they are spayed or neutered. It is better to wait until they are older, but they should be spayed or neutered no later than nine months of age.

Kittens should be spayed or neutered before they are adopted. Humane societies and shelters have found that many people adopt the pets with the understanding that they are to be spayed or neutered at an appropriate age, and pay a deposit to be refunded when the event has taken place, but fail to have the pet altered. Sometimes it just seems inconvenient or they do not want to "hurt" the pet. That is why many pet adoption agencies are now having the pet spayed or neutered before adopting. It does not make sense to place an animal in a home, and have four or five offspring of the animal returned to the agency for adoption within one year.

Step Two: *Get a trap*

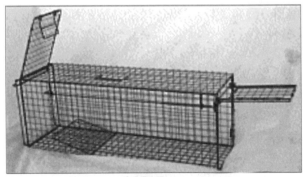

30D Trap
Picture with permission of Heart of the Earth Marketing

A trap can be rented or purchased. It is a good idea to rent a trap at first, but if you are serious about helping stray and feral cats, it may be cheaper and/or more convenient to buy a trap. Traps can be rented from some humane societies as well as local organizations that help cats and/or other animals. Some hardware and pet stores also rent traps. If you do not have a local source to rent or borrow a trap, you may have no choice but to buy.

Buying a Trap

Traps can be bought at some pet and hardware stores, by mail order or the Internet. Two companies that sell the traps directly and in several sizes are:

> Heart of the Earth Marketing, Distributor
> Tru-Catch Animal Traps
> 205 High Street
> Fruitdale, SD 57742
> 1-800-526-1644
> Website: animal-traps.com

> Tomahawk Live Trap Company
> PO Box 323
> Tomahawk, WI 54487
> (715) 453-3550 or 1-800-27-A-TRAP
> Fax (715) 453-4326
> Website: LiveTrap.com

Suggested trap size is approximately 26 x 9 x 9 or 30 x 9 x 11. These sizes are meant for cats and other similar sized animals, and are lightweight and sturdy. You will be taking the trapped cat to the veterinarian in the trap. (The prices for traps run about $45 to $50 plus shipping.)

Make sure the trap has a handle guard so the cat won't scratch you. Most have the handle guard included, but there is a lightweight trap that has the handle guard as an extra. This is a metal piece around the handle with which you carry the trap. This keeps the cat from scratching you. This is important. The cat is wild and frightened. It is not a pet!

Buying Versus Renting the Trap

Analyze the cost of renting versus owning before deciding which way to go.

In some areas, traps can be borrowed for free. However, I have had to pay from $5 for 10 days at a local humane society to $5 per *day* from a hardware store. There was also a deposit in both cases.

In addition to the cost of renting, there is the time and money you spend going to and from the place where you rent or borrow the trap. I finally bought a trap after trapping three kittens and a mother with a rented trap. I got tired of taking the trap back and forth, having to come up with the deposit, and worrying if I would trap within the allotted time (that has not really been a problem; it has never taken me more than two days of trying to trap, but you don't always trap the first time out).

Back to the cost, at $5 per day I think that buying a trap would work out as the best way to go in the long run. At $5 for 10 days, it may be cheaper to rent the trap, especially if you do not have a lot of space to store things, or do not plan on trapping many cats. The main reason I put off buying the trap was lack of storage space. But the inconvenience of renting, and not having a rental trap available the last time I needed to trap convinced me it was time to buy a trap.

Step Three: *Get vouchers or an assistance group pledge if needed*

Before you actually trap the cat, find out about getting financial assistance if you need it. Call the humane society in your area or the local shelter. They usually either offer assistance or will give you telephone numbers of organizations that help with spay and neuter costs. Or look in the appendix in the back of the book.

Usually, you need to have this help in the form of a voucher or assistance either mailed to you or to the veterinary hospital before you take the cat in for surgery.

The assisting organization usually wants a description of the cat. Give a vague description and include all the cats you want to trap. This may be hard if you are not sure which one(s) you will catch and you cannot get as many vouchers as you may need. The veterinarian may be okay with having the description not matching the cat you bring in closely if he or she is aware the cat is feral.

Step Four: *Have a veterinarian lined up who treats feral cats*

Not all veterinarians handle feral cats. It is best to find a veterinarian who will take feral cats and is used to treating them. Again, your local humane society or other organization may be able to give you the names of veterinarians who work with feral cats.

My veterinarian who works with feral cats allows me to bring them in when I catch them anytime during the hours they are open. No appointment is necessary. If it is evening and they are still open, I take the cat over and the cat spends the night and is spayed or neutered the next day. If I trap the cat after they are closed, I put the cat in the trap in the garage or other safe space where the cat won't be bothered by other cats. I put newspaper or paper under the trap, and a towel or other cloth over the trap to make the cat more comfortable. I then take the cat in the next morning and it will be operated on the same day. I try to get the trap back when I bring the cat in if possible so I can either trap another cat or return it to the owner if it is a rental. I also bring along a regular pet carrier to bring the cat home in. The pet carrier is easier for me to get the cat out of at home.

Step Five: *Prepare to trap the cat*

Patience is the main ingredient to trapping, along with finding the appropriate bait.

The only way a cat is going to go into the trap is if he or she is really hungry. Feral cats are suspicious and will not usually go into the trap just because they are curious. This means you must withhold food from all cats if there is more than the one you are trying to trap. At first, I usually withhold food when I set the trap out, not at the prior meal. Since the feral cats I feed only get dry food, canned cat food is very appealing to them.

You need to set the trap when you will be around for a while. I set the trap in the morning and see if I trapped a cat before I go to work. Since the veterinary hospitals in my area do not do surgery on the week-ends, I do not trap on those days. I don't like to leave the cat in the trap for any longer than necessary. However, I do try to trap on Sunday evening to take the cat to the veterinarian on Monday morning.

I set out the trap when I get home from work and check it every 15 or 20 minutes to see if I have caught a cat. Some traps make a noise you can hear when the trap sets. As soon as a cat is caught, I go out to get the trap and put it in the garage with a newspaper under it to protect the floor and a towel over the trap to calm the cat. I do not want the other cats to realize that they might be caught in the trap and become trap wise.

I do not have much trouble with the cats I have previously caught going into the trap instead of the new cat. Once cats are trapped, they become much harder to trap a second time. This is why it is important to get the cat her shots and whatever else you feel is necessary while she is at the veterinarian's. You may never be able to trap the cat again, or the cat may leave for another area. However, all the cats I have trapped and released have stayed around, although I may not see them for the first day or two.

Trapping also makes them more suspicious of the person who trapped them. If the cat was becoming less wild, it may now revert to a more fearful behavior temporarily.

Step Six: *Setting the trap*

To set the trap, I find the easiest way is to put the can of food or whatever bait you are using in the trap first, and place in the back of the trap beyond the triggering mechanism. I usually put it on a table height surface (my washing machine does nicely) and carefully set the trigger mechanism. To learn to set the mechanism, ask them to demonstrate for you where you rent the trap or follow the manufacturers instructions if you purchased the trap. Then, being careful not to jar the trap and trigger the mechanism, set the trap in the location you have chosen.

Put the trap in or near the area where you normally feed the cat(s). Put a towel or cloth over the trap. Then walk away and be patient. (Although I have caught many cats without covering the trap, it seems easier when a towel or other cloth covers the trap. After you catch the cat, covering the trap will calm the cat.) I have found there is no way to speed up the process, let the cat take her time. If you go out and startle the cat, she will only be more suspicious and take longer to trap. Fortunately, cats do have a sense of curiosity as well as hunger.

A cat may go into the trap, eat the food and walk out again without setting the trap. Don't give up. More than one cat I have eventually trapped has gone in and eaten all the food in the can (I set out a whole can of food) and walked back out. If this happens, just put the trap away until the next feeding or the next day. Then set the trap out again. Keep setting the trap out—do not give up. As the cats get used to seeing the trap, they usually get less suspicious and eventually do go in to get the food. If the cat does not get trapped and eats the food, she will be back the next time you set the trap and each time it will feel safer until she finally springs the trap and you catch her.

If the cat(s) do not go in after two times setting the trap out, try new food or a new spot. Or don't put out food until the cat gets trapped. However, do feed the cats again after one day of not feeding. You do not want to jeopardize the other cats' health for the sake of trapping one cat. Try putting something smelly like tuna fish or sardines in the trap if the canned food does not work. If they do not eat it, throw it out and start with new bait the next time. If you set the trap out in the evening, it doesn't hurt to leave it until late. However, I don't leave the trap out overnight since there are skunks in my neighborhood and I definitely do not want to trap one of those!

Check on the trap every half hour or so, preferably from a window or at a distance. The less you disturb the trap, the less time it will take to trap the cat.

> *Some cats are more difficult to catch than others. While trying to catch one small female cat, who comes in my yard but spends most of her time at my next door neighbor's, I have instead trapped three other cats, two of which I had never seen before. They probably eat in my yard when I am not there, but I will never know for sure. The three cats were spayed (one) and neutered (two). Your trapping results may be successful, but not what you planned.*

Step Seven: *Taking the cat to the veterinarian*

When you catch the cat you want to have spayed or neutered, it is advisable to take the cat to the veterinarian as soon as you can. If you cannot take the cat to the veterinarian right away, take the cat as soon as possible to a quiet place such a service porch or garage where she will not be disturbed. Put a towel or other cloth over trap and if possible, put trap where other cats cannot see it. This will keep the other cats from becoming trap wise.

Some trapping instructions say it is okay to leave the cat in the trap for a day or two, but personally I like to get the cat out of the trap within twelve hours.

You should have a veterinarian who will work with you lined up first. If you are going to trap more than one cat, I suggest you try to explain what you are doing with the veterinarian who will work with you, and let you bring the cats in without an appointment or will give you some leeway with an appointment until you are able to trap the cat.

If you plan on trapping and releasing feral cats over time, you may want to choose a veterinarian that will do the spay and neutering at a reduced rate, or will accept the vouchers or other financial help you obtain from pet assistance organizations.

When transporting the cat to the vet, place a towel or newspaper under the area where you will put the trap in your vehicle. Leave the towel on the trap and carry the trap by the handle, keeping the trap away from your body. Remember, this is a wild animal and can scratch. The cat may bounce around in the trap but just hold the trap by the handle only and keep it as steady as you can while keeping the trap at a safe distance from your body.

When you get to the veterinarian, put the cat in its trap as far away from the other animals and people as possible. Leave the towel over the trap as it helps to calm the cat. The cat looks like a pet, and some people may want to touch it. I stay close to the trap for that reason—to warn people to stay away.

When signing the cat in at the veterinarian's, let the receptionist know that the cat is feral. Ask to have dissolving stitches. It is a good idea to have the cat's ear notched or clipped so that you and others know the cat is feral and has been altered. Let the receptionist know of any special financial arrangements you have and have the paperwork with you if it was sent to you instead of to the veterinary hospital. In my area, most times it is sent to the veterinarian, which is why you need to arrange for financing and a veterinarian before trapping.

Decide what shots the cat needs and you can afford. If you are unsure what the cat needs, check with the veterinarian. Different areas have different needs for shots. Decide if the FelV/FIV test is needed. The immunization shots are pretty much a given; they are good if you can afford them. Most times, this is the only immunization the cat will ever get, so it is a one-time expense. But the FelV/FIV test is more expensive than the shots, and offers no benefit to the cat. The only reason for getting it is to have the animal put down if he or she tests positive. However, the test should be administered before a cat is adopted. An FIV or FelV cat should only be adopted into a single cat, indoor only household.

When it comes to a litter of kittens, the cost of spaying or neutering and the shots can add up pretty quickly. And none of that cost includes the food you feed them and your pet cats, if any, as well as the medical costs for your pet cats that at times runs into the hundreds of dollars per year.

I decided the best I could do for these cats was to not have them tested for FIV/FelV so I could get them spayed or neutered and their immunization shots. It

I was feeding a male cat who was relatively tame and, although altered, was very territorial and got into fights. I was able to put a disinfectant on his wounds when he got them, but then he got pretty beat up and did not look well. I got him into a cage and took him to the veterinarian. The veterinarian thought he looked unhealthy and wanted to test for FIV. It turned out he was positive. Because of his poor condition, she advised me to have him put down. I felt very badly as this was not my intention when I took him to the vet. Since I knew the veterinarian was against euthanasia in general, but suggested the cat should be put down, I knew it was for the best. This did not stop me from feeling terrible.

The next two cats I trapped I had tested for FIV because of that incident. I felt the disease could be in the feral cat population in my neighborhood. The cat that had FIV must have gotten it from another cat in the neighborhood that was possibly still at large. Both cats looked healthy and tested negative for FIV. What a relief! However, the one spay, one neuter, the shots and tests for both cats plus the rental of the trap set me back more than I could really afford.

Since that time, I have not had the FIV test done on healthy cats that I trap to be spayed and neutered.

was still a strain on my budget, but better than having lots of kittens each spring, watching and listening to the fighting over territory, and seeing them get run over or killed in other ways.

Many humane organizations believe the test is unnecessary for cats that will be released to their territory if the cat appears healthy. Killing cats that test positive does not remove the infection from the colony. If the cat is to be adopted, then she should have the test. You would not want to put a cat who is FIV positive into a home with other cats. If the cat is healthy but positive, it can be adopted into a home with no other cats and be kept indoors. FIV positive cats may lead healthy lives for a number of years. However, the decision of whether or not to put down an FIV positive cat is not an easy one. Many healthy cats without FIV are euthanized every day because they do not have a home. Why put a cat with a disease in a home when that same home could have a healthy cat? A difficult decision, and a decision that each of us must make for ourselves with the advice of our veterinarian.

Before leaving the cat with the veterinarian, find out when the cat can be picked up. Usually it will be the day after surgery. The veterinarian may give you a sheet for after surgery care; if not, ask what you need to do to help the cat's recovery.

Step Eight: *Releasing the cat after surgery*

Both males and females can be released the next day after surgery. However, it is better to have a few days of reduced activity if possible, especially for the females.

If possible, keep the cat confined for a day or two. I have a dog run, a chain link enclosure, 4 feet by 10 feet with chain link on the top as well as the sides. Cats can and do climb the day after surgery, so if you do want to confine her, the cage or other enclosure must have a covered top. I put the cat in the enclosure for two or three days after I pick her up from the veterinarian. That way, I make sure she gets food and water and does not get in a fight or strain herself. I can make sure she is doing well before releasing her. I also have a much better chance of re-trapping the cat in the enclosure than if I release her in case of complications. I put a small litter box in the enclosure. The enclosure has a roof over part of the chain link top to keep out rain and too much sun, a cat condo to sleep in, and dry food and water at all times. I put in a can of cat food once a day to spoil her a little.

I usually keep the cat in the enclosure for three days to make sure she is healed and to rest while she gets over the physical and emotional stress of the surgery and the trapping. The enclosure is in its familiar territory of my backyard, and most cats take it pretty well. This treatment is not necessary after surgery if the cat has stayed overnight at the veterinary clinic, but it is a nice precaution if you have a space available.

I bring the cat home in an animal crate. I put the crate inside the enclosure facing away from the entrance gate and open the door. The cats always take at least a few moments to leave the crate, which gives me time to get out of the enclosure and close the gate. Sometimes the cats will not leave the crate until I go into the house. Sometime later the same day, I go into the enclosure and remove the crate, being careful not to let the cat escape. I usually wait to do this until the cat calms down.

The first thing most of the cats do is climb over the entire enclosure looking for a way out. Then they calm down. I leave them alone since my presence causes them more stress, although when I am out there I tell them they will be okay and not to be afraid. I don't know if this helps, but I don't think it hurts any.

I usually leave the cats in for three days after they come home from the vet. However, one female cat was so stressed by being in the enclosure that I released her a day and a half after the return from the veterinarian. She was fine, and comes around every morning and afternoon at feeding time. I don't really think the three days is necessary, especially for males, but it is just a way to ensure the cat is fully ready to be returned.

If the spay or neuter is done in a harsh climate when it is very cold, I think it would be better to make sure the cat has a warm secure place for the first few days if possible.

After release, you may not see the cat for a few days or ever again for that matter. My personal experience is that all the cats I have trapped have returned to be fed. Perhaps it is because they are so territorial, or that food is hard to find. I am always happy to see them and know they are doing okay.

The cats will be more suspicious of you now that you have trapped them and taken them to the veterinarian. They may not let you get close to them for a while, and you may lose a lot of ground you have gained in the cats trusting you. But I am positive this is in the best interest of the cat, and if they are not as trusting, so be it. I have my pet indoor cats, all former homeless kitties, so I don't need the feral cats' gratitude; just knowing they are okay is enough.

The trap, spay or neuter and release process needs to be repeated with all new cats you are feeding. Each time you will learn what works for you and the procedure gets easier. If you don't spay and neuter and just feed the cats, you will be part of the cat population problem. The cats will multiply even faster when they are well fed and there will soon be too many for their territory. They will be stressed, get in fights, and will not be as healthy and happy as the altered kitties. And the population will keep growing.

Please be a responsible cat feeder. Trapping is not as hard as you think.

Taming Feral Cats and Kittens

*T*he decision to tame and adopt feral cats and kittens must be undertaken with great care. Cats are sensitive creatures, and to disturb them can cause great damage even though well intentioned.

We see feral cats with their fleas and leaner bodies and think they would be better off indoors getting fat and lazy like our housecats. But this is not better for all cats, and definitely not possible for all of them. At this time, there just are not enough homes for all the feral cats that are in the world even if they could all be tamed.

The best candidates for socializing are kittens between two and eight weeks of age. The problem with this is if the mother is truly feral, you probably will not see her kittens until they are at least ten weeks old, and she has already taught them to fear humans. This means that the majority of feral cats you encounter will not be good candidates for taming.

Stray cats who have been socialized at one time or another can be tamed more easily but may be difficult to tame as well.

When deciding whether or not to tame, first consider the temperament of the cat or kitten. If a cat is very shy and skittish, he will be more difficult to tame and may respond poorly to any changes after taming. A shy or skittish cat is never as tame as a more confident animal.

Before you decide to tame a cat or kitten instead of spaying or neutering and returning her or him back to the neighborhood, consider the consequences:

🐱 If you have a cat or cats, or wish to put the cat up for adoption, the new adoptee should be tested for FelV/FIV. If the cat is positive for one of the diseases, will you then return the cat to the wild knowing it may transmit the disease to others, or have him or her euthanized?

🐱 Do you plan to keep the cats yourself or put them up for adoption? Many times feral cats and kittens become attached to the person who tames them and may not adjust well to others.

🐱 If the cats are adopted and do not adjust well to their new homes, what will happen to them? Will they be turned into a shelter where they stand a good chance of being euthanized? Will they then go to yet another home where they cannot adjust? Or will you take them back? How many cats can you keep as pets where you live? And can you afford a number of cats?

You may fail to tame some cats, and have to return them to the wild in spite of your best efforts. What you think is best for the cat is not always what the cat feels is best or is capable of accepting. A cat that seems to be socialized can revert to wild behavior when placed in another home.

Kittens can be spayed and neutered at around four to five months of age (or as early as eight weeks if necessary or before being adopted) and returned to the colony. In many areas, including my own, almost all tame kittens that are turned into the local shelters are euthanized. With such a surplus of kittens, it may be wiser to return the kittens back to be with their littermates and relatives in the colony after being spayed or neutered and vaccinated unless you wish to adopt them yourself.

> *Kenny and Steve, my two former feral kittens, still run and hide when they hear someone knock at my door after being with me for four years.*

If kittens are orphaned or the mother and/or kittens are sick, and you want to try and save the kittens, then the kittens will be tamed while being medicated. There is really only the choice of letting the kittens die or taking care of them, which will tame them. The care of orphan kittens before weaning is covered in the next chapter.

Taming Kittens

Catch the kitten(s) you want to tame as early as possible after they are eating solid food, at six to seven weeks if possible. You can catch them with gloved hands if you can get near enough to them, or bait a trap. See the previous chapter for instructions on trapping. Kittens being so curious are easier to trap than adults.

The process of taming kittens takes two to six weeks depending upon:

- The age of the kitten(s)
- How wild the kitten(s) are
- The time you can devote to taming them

You must isolate the kittens at first. Separate each kitten from his or her littermates and other cats. This will help each kitten bond to you. Also, the kittens should be kept separate from any other cats you have until your veterinarian has checked them for disease and they have been vaccinated. Most feral kittens do not have immunities to disease from their mother since she was probably never vaccinated.

Be careful when handling the kittens. They can and will bite and scratch. Remember, they are cute but wild. If they are older, you may want to wear gloves while handling them until they become tame enough not to scratch and bite. If you do get bitten, take care of the wound immediately and seek medical help if needed.

If the kittens are nine weeks or older, you may want to have them spayed and neutered before you start taming. At the same time, they can have their first shots, get the FIV/FelV test, and get wormed. This gets all the traumatic events over, and you then can start building trust with the kittens. It also assures you that you have healthy kittens. FIV and FelV can be transmitted to the kitten from an infected mother.

Steps to kitten taming

Step One: *Confine the kittens.*

Confinement is necessary to allow the kittens to bond with you. Put the kitten in a small cage or large cat carrier with food, water, and some cat litter in a small container. Keep the cage in a small room if possible where the kitten will not be disturbed. Kittens can be in the same room but in separate cages. Visit the kittens and talk to them, but do not attempt to touch them for 24 to 48 hours. Move slowly and deliberately around them and speak softly. The kittens need to feel safe.

Step Two: *Handle the kittens briefly several times a day.*

Use a towel to place over the kitten and pick her up. She will probably hiss and spit at you. Stroke the kitten briefly with the towel or your hand and speak to her softly and reassuringly. Then put the kitten back. Do this for a very short period of time, no more than five minutes. Do it two or three times the first day, then increase the number of times the next few days and gradually pick her up and pet her for a longer period of time. A good time to do this is right before feeding. Try using the food to get the kitten to come to you. Then the kitten will associate petting with the pleasure of being fed.

Kittens need to be stroked. Their mothers lick them roughly with their tongue, and the stroking feels much like what the mother was doing for them.

Step Three: *Three to four days after you first confine the kittens, and they allow you to pick them up, you can put them back together.*

At this time, you may release them in a small room. Make sure they will come out when you bring food so you can pick them up, or that there are no places they can hide where you cannot reach them. The absence of hiding places is more critical if the kittens are sick and need medication. The handling should continue during this period.

Step Four: *After about a week have other people handle the kittens.*

Having the kittens get used to other people is very important to their socialization, especially if they are to be adopted into another home. Have other people pick them up and play with them. You can play with the kittens using cat toys or string that you do not leave with the kittens when you are gone.

Step Five: *When the kittens are tame enough, healthy and vaccinated, they can be released into a bigger room or part of the house.*

It can be overwhelming for the kittens to have too large of a space all at once. You may want to keep them in just two rooms at first. They can be released into the entire house, but don't be surprised if they stay in one area for a few days before exploring the rest of the house. Let them move out at their own pace, and if they hide for a while, that is okay.

This is when they will go to their new home if they are to be adopted. Ideally, the new owner would be part of the taming process, but this is usually not the case. Be sure and let the new owner know the kitten was feral, and that she must be treated carefully and may take some time to adjust to the new surroundings. Have an agreement with the new owner that the kitten will be returned to you if the adoption does not work out.

It is better if the kittens go to homes without children. The noise and sudden movements of young children can be disturbing to feral cats and kittens.

Some feral kittens will always be elusive and hide from strangers and run at sudden noises, etc. Others will bond very closely with their owners and be very affectionate. For an understanding owner, both kinds of formerly feral cats can make good pets.

Taming Feral Adult Cats

Taming feral cats older than six months can be difficult. Unless you feel strongly about the cat and want to adopt it yourself, I do not recommend it. Most cats prefer their freedom once they know it. However, sometimes a cat seems tame, you can pet him or her and he or she seems to want to come inside. If the cat is not too old and seems to be tame, especially if you can pick the cat up, it is not truly feral.

Consider your circumstances:

🐱 Do you already have other cats in your house?

🐱 Can you afford to have another pet financially?

🐱 Do you have enough space?

🐱 How will your other cats react?

🐱 Is it possible you can find the owner?

It is harder to introduce an adult cat rather than a kitten into a household. It will be stressful for both the new cat and the cat(s) that you already keep in your home. Tame cats under stress can revert to more primitive behavior such as marking their territory by clawing and/or spraying urine.

However, after looking at things sensibly you still want to adopt an adult feral cat, here are the steps:

Step One: *Trap the cat*

The trapped cat first needs to be spayed or neutered, given shots, tested for FelV/FIV, given an exam for general health, and optionally (although I think this is a must) be treated for worms and fleas. When you bring the cat home it should be placed in a cage if you have one with a blanket over it, or a very small room. The cat should be in a quiet place where it will not be disturbed. Have the food, water, and litter already in the cage or room when you put the cat in, or wait until the cat has calmed down before doing so. Any other diseases that the cat could have should show up during this isolation period. This protects other cats in your household. A two-week period should be adequate.

Step Two: *For the first few days, just replace the food, water and litter*

Talk softly and calmly to the cat while you are doing this. Otherwise, leave the cat alone.

If the cat seems calm while you are in the room, start sitting in the room with the cat. You can occasionally talk to the cat. Otherwise, just sit there but do not stare at the cat, because cats perceive staring as a sign of aggression. Look away from the cat for the most part. You can read or do something else. If the cat starts climbing the walls of the enclosure when you are there, she is not ready for this step.

Step Three: *Touching the cat*

Be prepared for this step. You may want to wear gloves, and be sure you have current tetanus shots. This should be done before you start trapping cats. If the cat seems calm reach toward the cat. If the cat remains calm with ears erect or to the side, gently touch the cat on the back area. If the cat puts the ears back, hisses or lunges, wait another day. The next time, offer a piece of food in one hand and try to pet the cat with the other hand. A piece of chicken seems to appeal to most cats. Take your time on this step. The cat cannot be rushed. If the cat is extremely shy, you may have to wait for a few days before trying again. Trust can be hard to build.

Step Four: *After a few days to one week of being able to pet the cat, you can let it out of the cage or the small room and into part of the house or the whole house*

If there are other cats in the house, you may want to keep them separate from the new cat for a week or two more. Do not be surprised if the former feral cat stays in one room for a while or hides out. This adjustment can take time.

The taming of an adult feral/semi-feral cat takes time and patience. You cannot move more quickly in the process than the cat can accept. A friendly, calm cat will socialize more easily than a shy skittish cat. At times, you may have to go back a step in the process if the cat becomes distressed for any reason.

Taming cats and kittens can be rewarding and they can turn into loving pets (I have four of them). Just be sure to have a plan for their eventual future before you go through the taming process, and that it is in the best interest of the individual cat you decide to tame.

Orphan Kitten Care

Kittens are always better off being cared for by their mother. It is only when a kitten is abandoned by the mother, or the mother and/or kittens are sick that kittens should be taken from their mother before they are weaned. If at all possible, leave the kittens with their mother until they are five to six weeks of age.

If orphan kittens are younger than five weeks old, you may want to try to find a foster cat mother. Veterinarians and animal shelters may know of potential foster cat mothers.

If you must foster and hand feed them before they are weaned, it will take considerable time, energy and patience, and money for veterinary care. You can become quickly attached to helpless sick kittens, and wind up spending a considerable amount for veterinary care in an effort to save them. Be aware that very young kittens may not survive without a mother no matter how good the care.

Be sure to have a veterinarian that you are comfortable with and trust on hand, for you will need his or her guidance at times, and for vaccinations at the appropriate age. If this is your first time caring for an orphan kitten, I suggest that you take the kitten to your veterinarian as soon as possible. Veterinary care should always be a consideration for your cats. The feral mother, if sick, may allow you to catch or trap her so you can get her veterinary help. But if she is sick and the kittens are not removed, whether she can be caught or not, the kittens will most likely not survive.

Feral mother cats can become sick with diseases for which most household cats have been vaccinated. Feral cats have no immunizations, and stray cats may not either because owners who desert cats often give them no care other than food. If the mother is sick, the kittens must be removed from her care. If the kittens are sick, they must be removed from the feral mother cat even if the mother cat is well so they can be medicated regularly.

Until the kittens are checked out by your veterinarian and pronounced healthy, they should be separated from other cats in your household. A two-week isolation period after the veterinary check is still advisable to prevent the spreading of contagious disease. Upper respiratory disease is common among feral kittens and is very contagious. Sick kittens that do not get medical care will probably not survive. If the kittens are not yet weaned, (less than six weeks old) they still may not survive even with medical care. Kittens are fragile, and many feral kittens die with or without our help. However, the kittens that are cared for by us make excellent candidates for adoption due to their interaction with humans.

What You Need to Get Started

- Nursing bottle and/or eyedropper
- Feline formula (from pet store or veterinarian) or goat's milk may be substituted
- Towels and washcloths
- Cotton balls
- Heating pad
- Room thermometer

Steps to Raising Orphan Kittens

Step One: *Get and keep the kittens warm.*

The first thing kittens that are under five weeks of age need is warmth. The mother cat and the other kittens keep the kittens warm, and kittens cannot generate much heat for themselves for the first few weeks of life. If chilled, a kitten's blood sugar level can quickly drop and the kitten's system will start shutting down.

Most feral kittens that are found are already losing body heat, and hypothermia may have set in. It is critical that the kittens be warmed immediately.

Put the kittens under your coat, sweater, or other clothing and next to your skin. Gently massage or stroke the kittens to increase circulation. Get the kittens to a warm environment as soon as possible.

Week old kittens need an environment of 88 to 92 degrees. For the next three to four weeks, they need a temperature of at least 80 degrees. You can lower the temperature a few degrees each week until 70 degrees is reached. At about five weeks, they can be in a lower room temperature, as low as 70 degrees.

When you reach where the kittens will be staying, put a heating pad on the low temperature setting or hot water bottle in a box or pet carrier on one side. Put a towel on the bottom of the box or carrier. Do not put the heating pad on the whole bottom of the box. The kittens need to be able to move away if the heat is too hot for them. Set the room thermometer in the room as well to make sure the temperature is correct for the kittens.

Step Two: *Take the kittens to the veterinarian.*

If possible, take the kittens to a veterinarian to be checked for dehydration and general health. Kittens can become dehydrated quickly when orphaned, and may need fluids under the skin. Dehydration must be taken care of as soon as possible, since a dehydrated kitten will not eat well and will not have much energy. Have the veterinarian check for worms, parasites, and fleas. Fleas can be very harmful to kittens, and the veterinarian will have an appropriate remedy to get rid of the fleas. The veterinarian will have some of the supplies needed as well as advice for raising the kittens.

Step Three: *Feed the kittens.*

Feeding can be done as soon as the kittens are warmed enough. Do not feed a cold kitten—this can kill the kitten. The kitten can be fed with a nursing bottle or eyedropper. Use the bottle if the kitten is able to suckle. Otherwise, use the eyedropper and slowly feed the kitten. Do not force feed. If fluid gets in the kitten's lungs it can kill the kitten.

Kittens must be fed every three to four hours. The formula should be warmed to body temperature, and all bottles and other equipment should be sterilized before each feeding to avoid disease. Wash your hands before and after feeding to avoid spreading any diseases to other cats or kittens. You may also want to use a waterless hand sterilizer product as an extra precaution. If kittens cannot seem to take in much food, feed more frequently, not more food at each meal.

To feed the kitten put her on a towel stomach down. This helps to prevent formula going down the kitten's windpipe. Try to keep the bottle at about a 45-degree angle to avoid air bubbles and keep a slight pull on the bottle to encourage suckling. If the kitten does get formula in its lungs, hold it upside down until it stops choking. Do not force feed or overfeed the kitten. Bubbles will usually form around the kitten's mouth when she is full.

After each feeding, burp the kitten. This can be done much like a human baby, by putting the kitten upright on your shoulder and gently patting on the back. Kittens can get sick and even die from too much gas.

After each feeding kittens must be stimulated to urinate and defecate. Dampen a cotton ball with warm water and use this to gently rub the abdomen and anal area until the kitten relieves herself. Then rub the kitten's fur all over with a barely warm damp washcloth or towelette in short strokes as a mother cat would to both stimulate and clean the kitten. This also gives the kitten a feeling of being wanted and cared for. This procedure needs to be done until the kitten can urinate and defecate by herself, usually around the third or fourth week.

If the kitten becomes dirty or has diarrhea and has caked stool, it is usually easier to bathe the kitten in warm water rather than to try and rub the offending matter off, which can be hard on the kitten's delicate skin.

Step Four: Weaning the kittens.

The kittens can begin the weaning process at about four weeks of age. Start by putting the kitten formula in a saucer or shallow bowl and let the kittens lap it up. Gradually introduce solid food, Hill's brand A/D or strained baby food, preferably all meat chicken or beef. Dry kitten food is best introduced after wet food. The dry food may need to be moistened at first. Look at the stool daily to make sure the kittens do not get diarrhea. This is especially important when you change foods, which can upset the kittens' digestive system.

Step Five: *Litterbox training.*

The kittens can be introduced to the litterbox at about four weeks of age. Try putting regular (not scoopable) litter in a cardboard box top, or cut down a cardboard box to a height that the kittens can get in easily (no more than two or three inches). Put the kittens in the box after each meal, and take each kitten's paw and show them how to scratch the litter if necessary.

Orphaned kittens are vulnerable to diseases. At the first sign of illness, take the kittens to see your veterinarian.

It is easy to get attached to kittens you care for. Please remember that orphan kittens may die in spite of the most careful care, especially if the kittens are less than three weeks old. If the kittens die, do not blame yourself. The kittens may have already had malnutrition or disease that made their death inevitable regardless of care. If the kittens survive and are healthy after they are weaned, they stand a very good chance of a long healthy life.

Long Term Cat Management

"Until we collectively abandon our first notion of attempting to tame and place or relocate every feral cat, we will continue to be 'behind the eight ball' in our efforts to get ahead of the game of feral cat overpopulation. And until we change our perceptions of what natural cat behavior is by believing that the only place they can be happy and safe is in a home or a barn setting, the more we will fall behind in our goal to reduce the overpopulation of feral cats and reduce the unbelievable number that are killed each day."

—Alley Cat Allies

Feral and stray cats make wonderful pets. The feral and stray cats in my neighborhood are proof that it is possible for feral cats to live a healthy existence and reasonably long lives without being indoors. The big question is how to manage the cat or cats over the long term. The answer is simple:

- Feed the cats high quality, nutritionally complete food

- Feed on as regular a schedule as possible

- Trap, spay or neuter and release cats or kittens that are you feed as soon as possible

- Have shelter and warmth for them if needed

Allow for Enough Time and Money

To help your feral cat or cats, you need to decide how much time and money you can afford to spend each time you consider adopting or caring for another cat. Check your resources each time you make a decision about a cat, whether it is a health need or adding an additional cat. You need to have the time and money on a consistent basis. You should also have an emergency fund for unexpected costs.

It does not take much time or money to feed a few feral cats on a regular basis. That is pretty much all they require. They do not need attention or taming unless you choose to do that. They have their own cat community.

It is a good idea to have a back up person to feed the cats if you have to go away from home. Often a neighbor or relative who is sympathetic to cats is willing to help out. Just like your pets, the feral kitties need to be fed and have fresh water every day. This is best thought of in advance, just in case of emergencies, just as you should have an emergency plan for your pets.

If you find that you wish to take on more cats than you believe you can handle by yourself, you might think about getting help, either through a cat assistance organization or a friend or relative. Do not take on more cats than you can handle! This does not help you or the cats. Remember, consistent daily care is the most important thing, not the one-time grand gesture. Living is a day-by-day adventure.

Shelter and Winterizing

If you live in a temperate area, the cat or cats may not need shelter. They do need a safe place to sleep. Like our housecats, they often find their own favorite safe places to rest.

Try to have a safe place for them to eat. The cats I feed eat in my backyard, which is fenced and dogs are therefore unable to get in and terrorize the cats (as well as eat all their food). Where the cats eat should be away from cars, people, and dogs that can disturb them. A fenced backyard is ideal. The fenced backyard also keeps the cats out of sight of neighbors who may be unsympathetic to cats. The cats are safer if they stay "in the shadows" and remain unnoticed.

If your winters are harsh, the cats need shelter. The shelter should protect the cats from getting wet, and keep them out of the wind and rain or snow. You can make a simple shelter out of plywood, or look around at yard sales and find a doghouse. I found an igloo style doghouse at a yard sale that is perfect for keeping the cats out of the wind and rain at a very reasonable price. The cats do not use it much, only on the very cold or rainy days. They prefer their own secret places, and that is okay. The shelter should be a few inches up off the ground so the rain cannot seep into it.

Health

It can be impossible to get feral cats to the veterinarian on a regular basis. We have to accept that we cannot always help them when they are sick and injured. They may not let us touch them, and may hide when sick or injured. Then we must accept that they must either get well or not without our interference.

We may be able to help if the cat is very sick or injured. The cat may allow us to pick it up and take it to the veterinarian. This is usually the only time you can help your feral cats medically. If you do pick up a sick feral cat, be very careful. Pick it up with a thick towel, and wear gloves and long sleeves, and quickly put the cat in a crate. A fearful cat is very likely to scratch and/or bite.

Normally, feral cats are healthy and do not need much medical attention. This could be because only the strongest feral kittens can survive.

If you can get medical help for a sick feral cat, the cat may be diagnosed as having a contagious disease. Then you must decide, along with your veterinarian, whether to try to cure the disease, which may include taming the cat so you can medicate it, or having to euthanize the cat to end her or his suffering and prevent the spread of the disease. Again, it is important to have a veterinarian who you can trust and has the same values concerning feral cats and the value of life that you do.

Neighbors and Feral Cats

Some of your neighbors may admire your efforts to help feral cats. However, some may not like cats, and consider the feral cats (and perhaps some pet cats as well) as pests.

Some of the neighbors that like cats may also be feeding feral cats. If they are not spaying and neutering the cats they feed, they are part of the cat over-population problem. You can help them by offering to trap the cats and take them to be spayed and neutered for them, and even pay if necessary if you can afford to do so.

You can try to educate them as well on the consequences of feeding without spaying and neutering. Educating people about the overpopulation problem is the best thing you can do in the long run. If people understand the problem they will be more likely to spay and neuter the cats they feed.

For the neighbors that are unfriendly to cats, I suggest keeping a low profile with the cats. Feed where people do not see the feeding (I think this is a good idea anyway). If you find that a person is friendly with you but does not have a good attitude towards feral cats, you may want to inform the person that you are actually trying to keep the population under control, explain that TNR is a proven solution to cat overpopulation, and that the cats help with rodent control. Seeing a number of cats congregating around food may lead unsympathetic people to believe that there are lots of cats in the neighborhood, whereas if they never see them, there will be no problem. You may also want to explain that the neutered and spayed cats do not make much noise, it is the unneutered cats that make noise while fighting and mating.

Managing your outdoor cats is easy. Feed regularly. Spay or neuter. Have shelter or a safe area available. Get medical attention if needed. By following these few simple rules you and your cats can enjoy many happy days.

Last Thoughts

Our outdoor cats, like our indoor pets, can become a part of our family. We learn to care for them, know their personalities, and worry about them at times. We have to learn to let them go as they grow and become independent, just as we do our children. We cannot protect them from life. We have to let them be free as they are meant to be.

Feral and stray cats deserve our help. And we can help. Helping is not about the 60 to 100 million homeless cats, it is about the one cat at your backdoor, or cats that you feed in your backyard. It is about trapping, spaying neutering and releasing one cat at a time. It is about feeding that same cat one day at a time. One person helping one cat one meal at a time.

Feral and stray cats have different personalities. Some can be sweet and affectionate, some greedy and aggressive. Some "talk" more than others. Some are shy, some want to make friends. Each cat is unique.

We have to understand for them that it is not the length of life that counts but the quality of that life. For the feral or stray cat, freedom with a regular supply of food is as good as it gets. Let us help them to live their life of freedom as comfortably and as long as possible.

Enjoy your outdoor pets. Listen to them as they greet you with meows when you go out to feed them. Watch them as they lie relaxing in the sun, or chase a butterfly or bug in your yard.

With only the small effort of setting out a bit of food, you have the opportunity to have one or more outdoor cats as pets. As an additional benefit, you have the knowledge that you are saving lives. These cats have no other resources.

When you set out their food every day remember to feel good about yourself for helping one of God's precious creatures.

Appendix A

Cat Rights

(Reprinted with permission of the San Francisco SPCA)

The growing popularity of cats as house pets has gone hand-in-hand with increased efforts to legislate, regulate, and even eradicate these animals from our midst. In light of this growing threat to cats' lives and welfare, we feel obligated to come forward and offer our perspective. The Cat Rights listed below represent the basic principles that have guided our efforts on behalf of cats. While each seems fundamental to us, these rights are far from settled: All except one reflect an intense controversy within the humane movement. We hope everyone will listen to all sides, participate in the debate, and reach their own conclusions—the fate of millions of cats depends on it.

1. **The Right to be recognized as a unique and important species.**

   The Debate: Everybody knows cats aren't dogs. But many people want to treat them as though they were. The nation's largest and most influential humane organizations, joined by powerful groups like the Audubon Society and state veterinary associations, are calling for new laws to regulate and control cats—laws almost entirely modeled on dog control laws enacted decades ago. Their reasoning? Only when cats are subject to mandatory license and confinement laws will they have the status they deserve.

Our View: Cats are unique and wonderful creatures, with unique needs, unique abilities, and unique problems. Subjecting them to dog control laws doesn't honor cats as a species or give them the recognition and respect they deserve. Even for dogs, these laws weren't meant to confer any beneficial status: They were and are a tool for protecting livestock, enforcing rabies mandates, and ridding the public streets of the perceived threat posed by unowned, free-roaming dogs. Once license laws were passed, unlicensed dogs became instant "outlaws," and literally millions have been impounded and killed as a result. Nor, in our view, are these deaths justified in the name of increasing the number of lost pets returned to their owners—a commonly cited benefit of mandatory licensing proposals. This goal could be accomplished with less cost in lives and dollars by simply promoting voluntary identification for pets. Punitive licensing and regulation schemes won't give cats—or dogs—the status they need. If we really want to help these animals, we believe we should focus on humane and compassionate ways to improve their lives.

2. **The Right to have their individual lives cherished and protected.**

The Debate: This principle seems so simple and fundamental, it's hard to believe it's controversial. But when it comes to stray, homeless, and feral cats, many humane organizations advocate not a right to life, but a right to death—albeit a "humane" death. In Miami

Beach, for instance, local residents vehemently protested a city plan to trap and kill homeless cats. These cat lovers offered to vaccinate and alter the animals, feed them on a daily basis, and provide veterinary care as needed. When they succeeded in getting a public hearing on the matter, one of the largest animal rights organizations in the country stepped in—not to support local cat lovers, but to urge Miami's mayor to go forward with the original "round up and kill" program. Life on the street is a hard, miserable life for a domestic cat, this organization said. Death, in their view, would be preferable.

Our View: We agree that homeless cats can face hardships, sometimes severe, and we wish every cat had a loving, responsible, indoor home. But we don't think less fortunate cats deserve to die. Death isn't the answer to a less-than-perfect life. And, in our view, there is little justification for the wholesale trapping and killing of healthy cats simply because no one claims to be the "owner," or because these animals lack the comforts of house pets and are exposed to risks that companion animals should not face. If an animal has a painful, incurable condition, if it has a fatal, contagious disease and cannot be isolated from others—these are cases where euthanasia may be justified. But to use death to ward off potential suffering, or to "solve" the problem of homeless and feral cats is not, in our eyes, a humane way to help cats or enhance their welfare. Life is too important, and to us the life of every individual cat is too important, to deal out death in such an easy fashion.

3. The Right to be free from cruelty and abuse.

The Debate: None! Everyone agrees cats have the right to be free from cruelty and abuse. And all states have enacted laws against deliberate animal cruelty. These laws may not always go as far as we like, and they may not always be interpreted as broadly or enforced as rigorously as we would want them to be—but the principle, at least, is well-established.

4. The Right to receive aid and comfort, including food, water, shelter, and medical care.

The Debate: Millions of abandoned cats are helped by compassionate people every day. Some of these people are organized and dedicated caregivers who provide daily food and water to colonies of feral cats, and who make sure their charges are altered, vaccinated, and given emergency medical care. Others are simply kind-hearted people who lend a helping hand to the stray cat at the door—a cat with a good chance of becoming the family pet. (Studies indicate that up to 30% of pet cats are adopted by their human families as strays off the street.)

Do homeless cats have a right to receive this aid and assistance? Not according to those who believe feeding feral or abandoned cats amounts to nothing more than "subsidized aban-donment"—even if the animals are vaccinated, altered, and monitored on a daily basis. And far from seeing cat caregivers as Good Samaritans, these same critics view them as misguided, even criminal, wrongdoers. One leading humane organization went so far as to urge a North Carolina prosecutor to apply criminal laws against animal abandonment to cat caregivers working to spay and neuter homeless cats in their area.

Our View: We believe compassion towards animals should be fostered and encouraged, not criminalized. Countless people, many of us included, became cat lovers only after a stray at the door won our hearts. We may not have known at first all there was to know about responsible pet ownership, the importance of spaying and neutering, or the challenges of managing a feral cat colony. But to condemn the first steps towards compassion and understanding would prevent millions of people from opening their hearts and homes to help cats. And, most unforgivable, it would deny to millions of cats the love, protection, and safety net of care these people provide every day of their lives. To us, asking whether cats have a right to this life-sustaining aid is like asking whether the victims of earthquakes, floods, fires, or war have a right to the assistance offered by neighbors, friends, and compassionate volunteers. Of course they do.

5. **The Right to a fair share of public resources for the care and treatment of companion animals.**

The Debate: In California, shelters reportedly take in about as many cats as dogs. Yet fewer cats than dogs are redeemed by their owners or adopted into new homes, and many more are euthanized. Why? The reason heard most often is that the community is to blame: People are irresponsible; they won't do the right thing; they treat cats like second-class citizens. What's needed, then, is more legislation: coercive legislation to compel the cat-owning public into caring—and caring the way the legislation's proponents want them to care—for their pets. Spay/neuter mandates, cat licensing ordinances, vaccination laws—all are being promoted as ways to help cats and all are focused on forcing others in the community to change their behavior through punitive government mandates financed by taxpayers.

Our View: When we look at the millions of people helping cats throughout the country, it's hard for us to blame the community. It's even harder when we see what's happening inside shelters themselves. In most of today's shelters—both public and private—dogs get the lion's share of time, space, and attention. During their stay, dogs are usually housed in runs, often with indoor/outdoor access. But cats are typically kept in steel cages stacked one on top of the other, sometimes in rooms that weren't designed to hold animals at all—conditions that readily invite the spread of disease. To deal with this threat of disease, welfare experts openly advise shelters to keep their cat populations down by killing cats and maintaining empty cages. With death, rather than fair and equal treatment, promoted as a legitimate "cure," it's little wonder more cats than dogs die in our country's shelters. What's harder to believe is that some choose to point their fingers at the community for treating cats like second-class citizens, rather than focusing on shelters who set the example.

6. **The Right to be treated as equal members of the animal kingdom.**

The Debate: The fact that cats are gaining in popularity as housepets hasn't kept them from being ranked among the "throwaways" of the animal kingdom. Feral, stray, and homeless cats, in particular, are seen as "pests" in our cities and towns and as "non-native" intruders in our parks and countryside. In either case, the point is clear: Their lives don't count, and therefore they can and should be eliminated to protect more important species and to preserve "natural" habitats and "native" environments. Park rangers, environmentalists, bird watchers, and even animal protectionists have endorsed cat eradication, most recently in the name of protecting songbirds. Cats kill birds, they argue, so we must kill the cats.

Our View: Cats aren't the first to be targeted for slaughter in the name of protecting other species or preserving "native" habitats. They've been joined at different times and in different places by red foxes, gulls, cowbirds, sea lions, coyotes, mountain lions, ravens, raccoons, wild horses...the list goes on. Referred to as "garbage animals," "alien" species, "weeds," and "vermin," these creatures have become scapegoats for the massive habitat destruction, environmental degradation, and species extinction caused by one species and one species alone: Humans. Had we honored and preserved life, had we treated all animals—cats, birds and every other creature who shares our planet—with the respect they each deserve, we might have spared many of the species now lost forever. To us, there are no "garbage animals" and slaughter and death aren't the tools we need to preserve life. To do that—to preserve the life of all animals—we believe we must honor and preserve the life of each.

7. **The Right to be represented accurately and humanely by those who speak on their behalf.**

    The Debate: Many have commented on a "strong cultural bias" against cats, and we don't have to look far to find cats portrayed in the worst possible light. Rather than being told of their beauty and grace, or of the companionship and affection they freely give us, we are presented, again and again, with an image of cats as destructive and harmful. They are decried as wanton and dangerous killers, each said to "stalk and kill several hundred small mammals and birds every year," and together responsible for the death of millions of birds "each day." They are demonized as disease ridden threats to public health, who spread rabies, "human plague," and "the black death." And, in a new twist for these environmentally conscious days, cats have even been compared to "oil spills" and "poisons in the environment."

Our View: Myths, misinformation, and malice against cats are nothing new. But the words and images above don't come from cat-haters: They are the words of self-avowed cat advocates and all are taken from articles and pamphlets produced by humane organizations and intended to influence other animal agencies and the public. Some of these publications were meant to encourage support for cat control laws. Others had a different message. But whatever the message, in our eyes the method of promoting it is just plain wrong. Everybody knows cats aren't perfect, and a balanced point of view is essential to educating pet owners to care responsibly for cats. But cats don't deserve the bad press they have gotten, and they certainly don't deserve it from those who claim to be acting in their best interests or speaking on their behalf.

Appendix B

Further Reading

Disposable Animals: ending the tragedy of throwaway pets, Craig Brestup, Camino Bay Books, 1997.

Save Our Strays: How We Can End Pet Overpopulation and Stop Killing Healthy Cats & Dogs, Bob Christiansen, Canine Learning Center Publishing Division, 1998.

The Silent Miaow, Paul Gallico, Three Rivers Press, 1964.

The Stray Cat Handbook, Tamara Kreuz, Howell Book House, 1999.

The Wild Life of the Domestic Cat, Roger Tabor, Arrow Books, 1983.

Video

9 Lives: Humane Feral Cat Management, San Francisco SPCA, 2001. A nine video set. Call the SF/SPCA at 415.554.3024 for more information.

Trap, Neuter, and Return: A Humane Approach to Feral Cat Control, Alley Cat Allies, 1999. www.alleycat.org

Websites

Amby's Feral Cat Information Page
   www.amby.com/cat_site/feral.html

Sue Freeman's Guide to Rescue Cats
   www.rescueguide.com

Love That Cat! Store
   www.lovethatcat.com
Has list of regional organizations that offer low cost
spay and neuter services for cats

Appendix C

Traps

Heart of the Earth Marketing, Distributor
Tru-Catch Animal Traps
205 High Street
Fruitdale, SD 57742
Telephone: 1-800-526-1644
Website: www.animal-traps.com

Tomahawk Live Trap Company
PO Box 323
Tomahawk, WI 54487
Telephone: (715) 453-3550 or 1-800-27-A-TRAP
Fax: (715) 453-4326
Website: www.LiveTrap.com

MDC Exports Ltd
Unit 11, Titan Court, Laporte Way
Luton, Bedfordshire LU4 8EF
United Kingdom
Telephone: 01582 6556000
Fax: 01582 613013
Email: mdc@mdcexports.com
Website: mdcexports.com

Appendix D

Supplies (crates, toys, trees, etc.) Mail or online

Doctors Foster & Smith
Telephone: 800.826.7206
Website: www.DrsFosterSmith.com

R.C. Steele Pet Supplies
Telephone: 800.872.3773
Website: www.rcsteele.com

Appendix E

Animal Organizations

United States, National Organizations

Alley Cat Allies
1801 Belmont Road NW
Suite 201
Washington, DC 20009
Telephone: 202.667.3630
Fax: 202.667.3640
Website: www.alleycat.org
Extensive feral cat information at Website. Also have books and video for sale. Feral Friends Network has names of caretakers.

Best Friends Animal Sanctuary
Kanab, Utah 84741-5000
Telephone: 435.644.2001
Fax: 435.644.2078
Website: www.bestfriends.org
Lots of information on feral and stray cats on Website as well as pet forum.

Doris Day Animal League
227 Massachusetts Ave., NE, Suite 100
Washington, DC 20002
Telephone: 202.546.1761
Fax: 202.546.2193
Website: www.ddal.org
Lobbying organization focusing on issues involving humane treatment of animals. Supports the trap, neuter and release program for feral cats, has booklet on feral cat care.

Feral Cat Coalition of San Diego
9528 Miramar Road, PMB 160
San Diego, CA 92126
Telephone: 619.497.1599 (local calls only)
Website: www.feralcat.com
Much information on Website about feral cats, many excellent articles on feral cats, assist with spay and neuter in local area (San Diego CA). Also assist with starting a program in your area.

Friends of Animals
777 Post Road
Darien, CT 06820
Telephone: 203.656.1522
Website: www.friendsofanimals.org
Dedicated to protect animals from cruelty. Has low cost spay and neuter program. Call 800.321.PETS for spay and neuter programs.

SPAY/USA
2261 Broadbridge Avenue
Stratford, CT 06614
Telephone: 203.377.1116 or 800.248.SPAY
Fax: 203.375.6627
Website: www.spayusa.org
A national referral service for affordable spay and neuter services. Call 800 number to be referred to a local clinic and have referral slip/certificate mailed to you.

Regional Organizations Helping Feral Cats

Advocates, Inc.
PO Box 4415
Kailua Kona, Hawaii 96745
Telephone: 808.326.3724
Email: flowers@kona.net
Website: www.enchantedfantasies.com/acats.html

Albuquerque Cat Action Team
PO Box 51683
Albuquerque, NM 87181-1683
Telephone: 505.323.2228
Email: mail@albcat.com
Website: www.albcat.com

Alley Cat Advocates
3020 Bardstown Road, #204
Louisville, KY 40205
Telephone: 502.634.8777
Email: contactus@alleycatadvocates.org
Website: www.alleycatadvocates.org

Alley Cat Rescue, Inc.
5830 Hagerman Road
Sarasota, FL 34232
941.378.0233
Email: Catnip5830@aol.com
Website: www.alleycatrescue.org

Ardmore Animal Care, Inc.
321 Carol Brown Blvd.
Ardmore, OK
Telephone: 223.7070
Website: www.ardmoreanimalshelter.org

Arizona Cat Assistance Team
PO Box J
Scottsdale, AZ 85252
Telephone: 602.840.9118
Fax: 602.667.3766
Email: azcats1999@aol.com
Website: www.azcats.org

The Bear Foundation, Inc.
Website: www.working4feralcats.org

Best Friends Catnippers
PO Box 55663
Sherman Oaks, CA 91403-5663
Telephone: 818.377.9700
Email: info@bestfriends.org
Website: bestfriends.org

The Branford Compassion Club, Inc.
PO Box 768
Branford, CT 06405
Email: dmlorella@snet.net
Website: pages.cthome.net/lorello/compassionclub/c
ompassionclubindex.html

The Cat Network, Inc.
PO Box 593026
Miami, FL 33159-3026
Email: info@thecatnetwork.org
Website: www.thecatnetwork.org

Cat Rescue, Inc.
2464 Laurel Cove Dr.
Virginia Beach, VA 23454-2056
Telephone: 757.496.9345
Email: catrescue@hamptonroads.com
Website: www.hrtide.com/community/groups/catrescue

Cat Rescue of Maryland, Inc.
Box 305
6400 Baltimore National Pike
Baltimore, MD 21228-3915
Telephone: 410.747.6595

The Catalina Island Cats
Email: elanjae@catalinaislandcats.com
Website: www.catalinaislandcats.com

Cat's Cradle
PO Box 2152
Harrisonburg, VA 22801
Email: catscradle@rica.net
Website: www.catscradlevirginia.com

El Paso Veterinary Medical Association Feral Cat
Program
PO Box 808
Santa Teresa, NM 88008
Email: epvma@epvma.org
Website: www.epvma.org/feral_cats.htm

The Feline Foundation of Humboldt County
PO Box 444
Arcata, CA 95518
Telephone: 707.825.7387
Email: info@ffohc.org
Website: www.ffohc.org

Feline Rescue Network
Website: www.felinerescue

The Feral Cat Alliance
PO Box 491214
Los Angeles, CA 90049
Telephone: 310.281.6973
Website: www.feralcatalliance.org

Feral Cat Coalition
17134 NE 84th Street
Redmond, WA 98052
Telephone: 425.883.7629

Feral Cat Coalition of Oregon
PO Box 82734
Portland, Oregon 97282
Telephone: 503.797.2606
Email: feralcats_Oregon@yahoo.com
Website: www.feralcats_Oregon@yahoo.com

Feral Cat Coalition of Portland
PO Box 82734
Portland, Oregon
Telephone: 503.817.7796
Website: www.teleport.com/~animals/feral.html

Feral Cat Friends of Central New York
PO Box 236
Weedsport, NY 13166
Telephone: 315.252.2406
Website: web.syr.edu/~sgsutlif/fcfhome.htm

Feral Cat Foundation
PO Box 1173
Alamo, CA 94507
Email: info@feralcatfoundation.org
Website: www.feralcatfoundation.org

Feral Cat Friends, Inc.
8255 White Oak Road
Garner, NC 27529
Telephone: 919.662.5365
Website: www.feralcatfriends.org

The Feral Cat House At The Animal Spirit
Website: www.theanimalspirit.com/catindex.html

Feral Cat Spay/Neuter Project
PMB Ste. D-5, #112
13619 Mukilteo Speedway
Lynnwood, WA 98037
Telephone: 206.528.8125
Email: fcsnquestions@hotmail.com
Website: www.spaycat.org

Fix and Feed Feline Feral Inc.
PO Box 270035
Tampa, FL 33688-0035
Telephone: 813.264.7571
Email: sharonsally@earthlink.net
Website: www.home.earthlink.net/~sharonsally/kitties

Fix Our Ferals
PO Box 13083
Berkeley, CA 94712-4083
Telephone: 510.433.9446
Website: www.fixourferals.org

Forgotten Felines of Sonoma County
PO Box 6672
Santa Rosa, CA 95406
Telephone: 707.576.7999
Website: www.forgottenfelines.com

Friends of Alley Cats of Tucson
Telephone: 520.850.0001
Email: rainbow_wildcats@hotmail.com
Website: www.petfinder.org/shelters/AZ16.html

Friends of Felines
PO Box 475
Castle Hayne, NC 28429
Telephone: 910.452.6721
Email: friendsofelines@aol.com
Website: home.ec.rr.com/friendsofelines

Friends of Feral Felines
Charlotte, NC
Telephone: 704.348.1578
Website: www.pixelforge.net/fff

Friends of Feral Felines
PO Box 8137
Portland, Maine 04107
Telephone: 207.797.3014
Email: mchase1@maine.rr.com
Website: geocities.com/mike17505

Greater New Haven Cat Project
PO Box 1432
New Haven, CT 06505
Telephone: 203.782.CATS
Email: GNHCP@netscape.net
Website: www.orgsites.com/ct/gnhcp

Habitat for Cats
Website: members.aol.com/habitatcat

Hawaii Cat Foundation
PO Box 10696
Honolulu, HI 96816
Email: HFC@hicat.org
Website: www.hicat.org

Island Cat Resources and Adoption
PO Box 1093
Alameda, CA 94501
Telephone: 510.869.2584
Website: www.icraeastbay.org

KitCat & Critter Rescue, Inc.
PO Box 5
Rohrersville, MD 21779
Website: www.kitcatrescue.org

M.A.M.A. (Mature Animals for Mature Adults)
PO Box 94
Prospect Harbor, ME 04669
Email: MAMA
Website: hammer.prohosting.com/~mama2000

Meow, Inc.
PO Box 999
Litchfield, CT 06759-0999
Telephone: 860.567.3277
Website: www.meow-inc.org

Meower Power Feral Cat Coalition, Inc.
PO Box 9696
Chesapeake, VA 23321-9696
Telephone: 757.399.0001
Website: www.geocities.com/meowerpower_99.geo

Metro Animal Resource Services, Inc.
PO Box 260077
St. Louis, MO 63126
314.962.4573
Email: info@metroanimal.org
Website: www.metroanimal.org

Metro Ferals, Inc.
PO Box 7138
Arlington, VA 22207
Telephone: 703.528.7782
Website: www.metroferals.org

Neighborhood Cats
2565 Broadway #555
New York, NY 10025
Telephone: 212.662.5761
Email: headcat@neighborhoodcats.org
Website: www.neighborhoodcats.org

Neponset Valley Humane Society
16 North Main Street
Mansfield, MA 02048
Telephone: 508.261.9924
Website: www.conejo.com/nvhs.html

Northeast Tennessee Feral Cat Network
PO Box 783
Blountville, TN 37617
Website: www.netal.org

O'Bryonville Animal Rescue
PO Box 9206
Cincinnati, OH 45209
Telephone: 513.871.PAWS
Email: info@theanimalrescue.com
Website: www.theanimalrescue.com

Operation Catnip
PO Box 90744
Raleigh, NC 27675
Telephone: 919.779.7247
Website: operationcatnip.org

Operation Catnip
PO Box 141023
Gainesville, FL 32614-1023
Telephone: 352.380.0940
Website: www.vetmed.ufl.edu.sacs/Catnip/index.htm

Palm Beach Cat Rescue and Humane Society, Inc.
292 South County Road, Suite 207
Palm Beach, Florida 33480
Telephone: 561.655.8245
Fax: 561.835.9088
Website: www.members.aol.com/PBCatRescu/index.
html

"PAWS", Inc.
PO Box 344
Harrisburg, PA 17108
Telephone: 717.957.8122 (voicemail)
Fax: 717.540.5813
Website: www.paawsofpa.com

PawsWatch Rhode Island Feral Cat Rescue
PO Box 3711
Newport, Rhode Island 02840
Telephone: 401.848.9TNR
Email: pawswatchre@aol.com
Website: pawswatch.org

PetPromise
PO Box 21091
Columbus, OH 43221-0091
Telephone: 614.878.8281
Email: petpromise@yahoo.com

Prince Georges Feral Friends
4203 Enterprise Road
Bowie, MD 20720
Telephone:
Website: www.pgferals.org/cats/pgferals.asp

Project Purr
PO Box 891
Santa Cruz, CA 95061
Telephone: 831.423.6369
Website: projectpurr.org

Purrfect Pals
230 McRae Road NE
Arlington, WA 98223
Telephone: 360.652.9611

Rehab-a-Cat
PO Box 3184
New Haven, CT 06515
Telephone: 203.787.5532
Website: www.bayarea.net/~stenor/rehabacat/

SADSAC
PO Box 972
Dumfries, VA 22026
Telephone: 703.221.0324
Website: www.sadsac.org

Safe Haven for Cats
270 Redwood Shores Parkway PMB #139
Redwood City, CA 94065-1173
Telephone: 650.802.9686
Website: www.safehavenforcat.com

San Francisco SPCA
2500 16th Street
San Francisco, CA 94103-4213
Telephone: 415.554.3000
Feral Cat Hotline: 415.554.3071
Website: www.sfspca.org

Silicon Valley Animal Rescue
PO Box 50249
Palo Alto, CA 94303
Telephone: 650.965.7827
Email: rescue@svar.org
Website: www.svar.org

Silicon Valley Friends of Ferals
Website: www.svff.org

The Smith Island Feral Cat Project
20967 Caleb Jones Road
Ewell MD 21824
Website: www.members.tripod.com/abcowebdesign

S.N.A.P. The Spay-Neuter Assistance Program, Inc.
Houston/San Antonio
Website: www.snaptx.org

Space Cats Club
PO Box 624
Cocoa, FL 32923
Telephone: 861.4858

Stray Cat Blues, Inc.
PO Box 8
Colmar, PA 18915
Telephone: 215.631.1851
Email: catnut@yahoo.com
Website: 222.petfinder.org/shelters/PA16.html
UNT Feral Cat Rescue Group

Campus Organizations Helping Feral Cats

Cal Poly Feral Cat Program
California Polytechnic State University
Email: acorns@in-con.com
Website: www.calpoly.edu/~tcanites/485

Campus Cats
Seattle, WA
Telephone: 206.524.7726
Website: unknown

Feral Cat Alliance of Texas
Dept. of Veterinary Anatomy &
    Public Health M.S. 4458
Texas A&M University
College Station, TX 77843
Telephone: 409.862.4569
Email: AFCAT@cvm.tamu.edu
Website: www.cvm.tamu.edu/afcat

Stanford Cat Network
PO Box 18287
Stanford, CA 94309-8287
Telephone: 650.566.8287
Email: catnet@forsythe.stanford.edu
Website: www.stanford.edu/group/CATNET

UNT Feral Cat Rescue Group
University of North Texas
Telephone: 940.565.0280
Email: dnewell@unt.edu
Website: http://orgs.unt.edu/feralcat/

The UT Campus Cat Coalition
The University of Texas-Austin
Email: jan.shrode@mail.utexas.edu
Website: www.ae.utexas.edu/cats

Canada Organizations

Alley Cat Friends Society
24165 Chief Lake Road
Prince George, B.C.
V2K 5L1
Email: Website: www3.telus.net/kozoris/alleycats/inde
x.html

Annex Cat Rescue
980 Yonge Street, Suite 905
Toronto, ON M4W 3V8
Telephone: 416.410.3835
Email: info@annexcatrescue.on.ca
Website: www.annexcatrescue.on.ca

Jazzpurr Society
The Herb Gray Centre for Non-Profit Excellence
Suite 205, 657 Ouellette Avenue
Windsor, Ontario, N9A4J4
Telephone: 519.258.9299
Fax: 519.258.3562
Website: www.wincom.net/JAZZPURR

Mississauga Animal Rescue Service
16-1375 Southdown Road, Box 326
Mississauga, Ontario L5J2Z1
Email: marsrescue@netscape.net
Website: www.simpatico.ca/marscats/

Street Cat Rescue Program
1635 Preston Avenue
Saskatoon, SK S7H2V7
Telephone: 306.975.3736
Fax: 306.343.0184
Email: catbuddy@quandrant.net
Website: www.quadrant.net/streetcar

Toronto Cat Rescue
PO Box 41039
Toronto, ON
M6B 4J6
Email: cats@druid.net
Website: www.druid.net/cats

United Kingdom Organizations

Caring For Cats
Website: www.caringforcats.org.uk/

Cat Action Trust 1977
PO Box 1639
London WB 7ZZ
Website: www.cat77.org.uk

Cats Online
Cats Protection League
17 Kings Road
Horsham
West Sussex
RH13 5PN
United Kingdom
Telephone: 44 (0)1403 221900
Website: www.cats.org.uk

Index

Order Form for Book

For U.S. and Canada, please send $14.95 plus $4.00 postage and handling for the first book ordered, and $1.00 postage and handling for each additional book. Other countries, please send $14.95 plus $8.00 postage and handling for the first book ordered, and $2.00 postage and handling for each additional book. Orders outside USA, send money order payable in U.S. dollars on U.S. bank only.

Name_____

Address_____

City_____ State_____ Zip_____

Quantity	Your Order	Amount
	Living in Shadows ($14.95)	$

Make check payable to: **Amythyst Publishing** P.O. Box 65021 Los Angeles, CA 90065-0021	Subtotal	
	Postage & Handling	
	CA residents add 8.25%	
	Total	

Quantity Buyers:
Discounts on this book are available for bulk purchases.
Write or call for information on our discount programs.

Ann Fisher is available for lectures or workshops on feral or stray cats. To contact Ann, email her directly at annfisher@ mindspring.com or telephone her at 323-259-9728.

Visit our website
www.LivingInShadows.com